Security and democracy under pressure from violence

Michel Marcus
European Forum for Urban Security
Paris (France)

Integrated project "Responses to violence in everyday life in a democratic society"

Council of Europe Publishing

French edition:

Sécurité et démocratie à l'épreuve de la violence

ISBN 92-871-5201-2

Cover: *Le monde familier* (1958), oil on canvas painting (50 cm by 60 cm)
René Magritte (1896-1967), JAOS collection, Mexico
Photo @ Arturo Piera

Design: Council of Europe Graphic Design Workshop

Council of Europe Publishing
F-67075 Strasbourg Cedex

ISBN 92-871-5202-0
© Council of Europe, July 2003
Reprinted October 2004
Printed in Germany

"... violence claims always to be counter-violence – that is, retaliation for the violence of the Other".

Jean-Paul Sartre
Critique of dialectical reason

Integrated project "Responses to violence in everyday life in a democratic society"

All Europeans feel affected by violence and its repercussions. Personal security is threatened every day in a whole range of places and circumstances: at home, at school, at work, at sports events and on the streets. While violence and the fear of violence affect everyone's quality of life, certain groups – such as women, children and the elderly as well as migrants, refugees and particular ethnic groups – may be seen as specific targets.

The integrated project "Responses to violence in everyday life in a democratic society" was launched by the Secretary General of the Council of Europe as a means of mobilising the Council's resources over a period of three years (2002-04) to address the widely shared concerns that violence engenders. Its main aim is to help decision makers and others to implement consistent policies of awareness-raising, prevention and law enforcement to combat violence in everyday life. Significantly, these policies have to be formulated and applied in ways that respect human rights and the rule of law. That is an absolute prerequisite for achieving lasting improvement in the actual situation and in people's feelings about security in Europe.

Security and democracy under pressure from violence is the fourth of a series of publications for a general readership containing recommendations or instruments used to launch Council of Europe activities and projects on violence prevention. The series also includes discussion and summary documents on the different topics covered by the integrated project.

CONTENTS

FOREWORD

It is through practical measures that the fundamental rights provided for in the Convention for the Protection of Human Rights and Fundamental Freedoms, and the principles of the rule of law and parliamentary democracy are incorporated into the daily lives of all European citizens.

It is now a priority and a political duty to use pragmatic means in order to address the major challenges to these fundamental rights and principles in present-day Europe.

This is particularly true of violence in everyday life, which is now of serious concern to all governments and citizens. There is an urgent need to introduce preventive measures and appropriate policies, both on paper and in practice.

This is the thinking behind the initiative I took in launching the integrated project "Responses to violence in everyday life in a democratic society" (2002-04), a complex undertaking entailing both analysis and action.

Security and democracy under pressure from violence strikes me as a major contribution to the debate, which, as we know, concerns democracies throughout Europe. Indeed, it both takes stock of the situation and serves as a starting point.

I consider that, more than ever before, it is the Council of Europe's raison d'être to serve as the ideal pan-European forum, where not only member states but also other European and international organisations can share their experience and enhance their political action at various levels. This is, to my mind, an ideal means of ensuring that European integration and the efforts it implies take on a tangible form for each of Europe's 800 million citizens.

Walter Schwimmer
Secretary General of the Council of Europe

9

I. THE FACES OF VIOLENCE

The spiral of suspicion and anxiety

European societies are trying to make sense of the changes they are undergoing; our values are being obsessively and painfully re-examined. The extraordinary improvement in our economic situation no longer assuages our anxiety and doubt. Terrorism, industrial accidents and resurgent epidemics are taking us into an era of great dangers.

Security has become a many-faced monster dominating debate in European democracies. During every electoral campaign political debate centres on insecurity and it is easy for political extremists to exploit the issue by caricaturing it. Democrats dread any event that demagogues might interpret for their own ends to justify their challenge to the present order. Extremist proposals are attacking our most firmly established legal principles head on.

We are no longer simply in an area of violence and crime, but an environment suffused with collective fears and anxieties. National situations, the future of Europe and globalisation provide the context. Industrial accidents, migratory upheavals, health problems, the corruption of some leaders, the negative effects of the introduction of market economies and terrorism are just some of the components of an insecurity which is finding expression in dangerous simplifications and the search for scapegoats. Nomads, foreigners, Roma/Gypsies and people from little-known countries are seen as the greatest of threats in this land of illusions, and Europe is experiencing a serious rise in racially-motivated acts of aggression. Even young people seem to be a danger, the source of every evil in an ageing society which perceives their demands and turbulence as violence and aggression.

Has Europe become an area of intolerance? Is the European Union triptych of freedom, security and justice already outmoded? Is security eating away at freedom and justice?

Every manifestation of a phenomenon fuels the constant testing of our ability to tackle it. Talking about organised crime raises awareness about a phenomenon that was for long underestimated, but also demonstrates our inability to deal with it. The opaqueness naturally cultivated by this type of crime adds to the anxiety. The legitimacy of a few international institutions suggesting reasoned approaches to the problem is not taken into consideration.

Now terrorism has been added to this bleak situation. The field is now open to the most demagogic, the most senseless types of discourse. After all, books maintaining that the New York attacks did not involve airliners have become bestsellers.

The speeches made by the heads of institutions often fuel this regrettable spiral of suspicion and anxiety. Demagogic impulses and the temptation to attract the media spotlight lead people to dramatise events and offer interpretations whose basic premises are never verified. The inadequacy of international research on crime is regrettable, the failure of politicians to take into consideration existing research is still more so.[1] The issue of immigration is a good illustration of such extreme attitudes. The essential link that has to be made between our economies' natural need for immigration, the need for free circulation of labour if we want to create a Europe of and for people, and the crime problems that may arise as a side effect of these policies is all too rarely established. When one looks at national statistics, one is stupefied to see how little foreigners figure in them. Combating a criminal economy that is trying to exploit migratory movements by organising illegal immigration and multiplying sexual supply by exploiting human beings in distress requires determined policies and cross-border co-operation, but certainly not a scandalous conflation of foreigner and criminal. The leaders of countries that "export" labour sometimes feel they are abused in domestic debates but have no possibility of replying. The repeated imprudence of public statement sometimes adds to the hysterical climate developing in Europe.

Doubts

If everything is becoming a source of anxiety, is it because our institutions and our technical and political leaders are no longer able to control, curb or reduce these phenomena? Should the system of insurance we have adopted in our private lives be extended to every domain, including those that are collectively managed?

Internal government agencies have for a long time been responsible for the problem of violence. According to Max Weber, citizens give the state the function of ensuring their security and, for this purpose, confer upon it the monopoly of violence. It is increasingly apparent that this model is now under serious challenge.

There is doubt about the ability of democracy to bring internal or external peace. Democracies also wage unjust wars. The idea that trade, science and culture inevitably lead to democracy has been called into question. The idea that our violence has been civilised or tamed by the evolution of moral standards, institutions and the economy is faltering.

Some countries are emerging from the communist era with difficulty, and this difficulty finds expression in a state that is particularly weak with respect to security functions and therefore the monopoly of violence. The proliferation of gangs and Mafia-like groups that carve up territories and take charge of security within them for the benefit of their own activities is a sign of the weakness of the state. The corruption of political leaders adds to the discredit of the state. In most developing countries, international aid is linked to the establishment of criminal justice models inspired by the northern countries. The World Bank has a programme to ensure

---

1. Philippe Robert and Laurent Mucchielli, *Crime et Sécurité, l'état des savoirs*, Editions La Découverte, Paris, 2002.

the security of commercial transactions through minimum legal regulations and *ad hoc* courts. The little use local people make of those courts and policing arrangements and their suspicion of them leads one to wonder if they are relevant to the needs of the population, who continue to use more traditional methods of settling disputes, including the summary execution of offenders.

When one looks at the nature of the international aid that treats all countries and cultures as if they were identical, it is astonishing to see how many west European experts from countries that are having enormous difficulty harmonising their legal systems nonetheless reach consensus as to what other countries should do. These countries then find themselves working with judicial systems based on prison just like the most classic western systems, with the negative results with which we are familiar.

Let us remember the advice of the Beninese philosopher Hountondji:

> Given the plural nature of every society and the remarkable ability of cultures to accommodate and/or take on new values, what, in general, are the factors that accelerate or hinder such developments? Moreover, what means can be used to optimise these developments without harming a culture's identity, and ensuring that the new values are internalised rather than experienced as being of foreign origin?[1]

The Secretary General of the Council of Europe said at the European Union Regional Conference on Conflict Prevention at Helsingborg (August 2002) that our capabilities in conflict prevention and peace-building were directly linked to the values we defend. In order to increase stability and prevent conflict we should not simply help build democratic institutions, but encourage the appropriation of our values by all sections of society. Mr Schwimmer went on to say that the Council of Europe had this kind of know-how and could also contribute to the fight against terrorism.

The background of democracy might be the culture of peace promoted by Unesco, the culture born of our diversity that respects human dignity and wishes above all to confront violence with lucidity and fairness.

The world changed radically after the Holocaust. Violence and horror no longer surprise us. History must be part of the democratic debate on violence. We should adopt an approach that helps us to secularise our violence, place it in its historical context and elucidate the degrees to which we accept it.

The duty of memory

European nations believe they experience their violence, fears and anxiety within their borders. Citizens believe they experience them in their immediate environment. Everyone forgets the globalisation of fears and violence and the globalisation of reactions and what they believe they experience in a limited area is simply the shock wave of fears and violence coming from elsewhere. The shock waves mingle and accumulate, hampering every effort to localise and establish the cause.

---

1. Paulin Hountondji "Brainstorming – or how to create awareness of human rights" in *Taking action for human rights in the twenty-first century*, Unesco 2000.

The tendency to hunch up over one's fear isolates individuals, so fear of terrorism does not bring people together: "It strikes other people and what I must do is take care that it does not strike me," people say to themselves.

Nations and individuals confront violence without memory, with no memory of the violence they have experienced or of their own violence.

The founding of the Council of Europe indicated the will of European countries to escape a logic of confrontation, war and violence in order to build the Utopia of an area of freedom and dialogue in which custom and civility would no longer depend on the use of violence. Utopia remains a Utopia, confrontations between states have waxed and waned. Violence is still with us, but the context has changed.

Sixty years on, the Council of Europe feels the need to re-examine the problem of violence by introducing a transversal programme on violence and implementing it in conjunction with another programme on the development of democracy. The two themes are closely related. Democracy is the most developed form of exchange, dialogue and free discussion. At the dawn of philosophy, Plato presented the search for truth through dialectics and opposed the "might is right" incarnated by the sophists for whom, it has been said, right was based on the most likely, but above all, the most politically useful reality, with in the background, as was then possible, the use of force, irrationality and violence.

The Council of Europe's initiative, "Responses to violence in everyday life in a democratic society", should help us to talk about our violence in the contemporary context of international crises, terrorism, and economic and social upheaval, elucidate the factors that have altered the course of violence in recent years and at the same time analyse everything that has changed in our perception of it, our way of presenting it and also of condemning it, in short, to find the meaning of this many-faced violence.

This is necessarily an international task since it is connected with our civilisation, the civilisations of which Europe consists. The idea that we can do this alone is obsolete. "Peaceful optimism is now based on the interdependency and globalisation that mark the victory of an individualist economic society over the political and military state".[1] This peaceful confrontation should take place without any type of moralising anathema.

The speeches of the president of the United States pointing the finger at "rogue states", the planet of evil states, advocating the struggle of good against evil in the temporal order, show clearly the danger warlike crusades to eradicate violence may lead us into. If there is one thing that all religions and philosophies teach us it is that evil and violence are in each one of us and that what Georges Bataille referred to as the "the cursed part" is also part of our humanity.

---

1. Pierre Hassner,"Par-delà le totalitarisme et la guerre" in *Esprit,* December 1998.

Violence, crime, terrorism and insecurity

Such uncertainties about our future and ability to remain lucid are found in our most domestic debates. This threat is fed by every threat, and surveys on the feeling of insecurity reflect the image of a bubbling cauldron in which past and future mingle, and near and far are mixed. Our words are taken from these fevered minds, the confusion that sometimes overtakes our freedoms and rights, this maelstrom of warnings, alarms and disaster scenarios. Sociologists pronounce on law, lawyers are economists, philosophers are ministers, criminologists are journalists. Images are abundant, words superficial.

Violence

The categories of criminal law do not tell us everything about the extent of violence. Lawyers and statisticians tell us that violence includes attacks, of whatever degree, on individuals, including murder, armed attacks and sex crimes. The first comparative studies of European statistics were based on this. It is easy to agree that the choice is arbitrary. Our insecurity is fed by many forms of violence. Throughout the 19th century, law and justice contained, managed and defined violence. What was not within their ambit was a matter of war, sedition, secret services and the country's foreign policy. Violence has outflanked law; countries no longer declare war, but the globalisation of violence is sweeping away our intellectual categories. Violence is becoming independent. Everything is becoming immediate violence with no history, immediately subject to the response of our criminal justice systems.

So much crime requires a legal approach, so much violence plunges us into examining the functioning of society and political positioning. The World Health Organisation attributes the violence of our societies to the stresses exerted on human nature by external social, economic and cultural factors.[1] "In the final analysis, the extreme diversity of what may be termed violence almost always comes down to a boiling over, an excess, an immoderation that destroys, or at least suspends, controlled and regulated forms of action and interaction. Violence is the deregulation of things and relations, the eruption of the unforeseeable, it is chaos."[2]

There is perhaps an urgent need to accept that "the dream of unity and the nightmare of anarchy",[3] of domination, will never leave us, rather than pursue the impossible eradication of violence.

Crime

Crime has also lost its content. The opening of the European economic market has internationalised a part of our internal crime. Europe is being built upon trade. Attempts to divert some of the wealth for the benefit of a few concern only crumbs

---

1. *World report on violence and health*, World Health Organisation, 2002.
2. Yves Michaud, *Changements dans la violence, essai sur la bienveillance universelle et la peur,* Editions Odile Jacob, Paris, 2002.
3. Pierre Hassner, op.cit.

of that trade, crumbs that have fallen from the banquet table at which the rich countries of Europe are seated. "Grey" or black economies always live on the overabundance of traded goods, and thefts account for the majority of offences. The internal crime we have experienced is being transferred to the international arena with most offences involving the appropriation of goods.

Such internationalisation has come to be called organised crime or serious crime. Prudence is required. Europol was established to deal with "organised crime". After much reflection, it reorganised its work around the idea of "serious crime", a notion that avoids discussions about the content of organised crime, especially violence.

The gradual unification of European countries and therefore their problems leads all acts involving several persons of different nationalities acting in several European countries and challenging common laws to be considered organised crime. "Organised crime group" shall mean a structured group of three or more persons, existing for a period of time and acting in concert with the aim of committing one or more serious crimes, in order to obtain, directly or indirectly, a financial or material benefit."[1]

In its annual report, Europol speaks dispassionately of the hierarchy of serious crime by placing "crimes against persons" in fourth position, where only illegal immigration is found.[2] Ultimately, all financial and economic offences will have to go into this category and thus be removed from the national sphere. The first transfers took place in relation to drugs and they are now being followed by immigration, trafficking in human beings and illegal capital transfers, with illegal trafficking activities and unlawful acts committed by multinationals such as Enron bringing up the rear.

There will always be neighbourhood crime in our cities. This type of offending is linked in many ways to serious crime which needs support areas, especially for recruitment purposes.[3] But it is being treated autonomously, if only through the development of specific policing and judicial methods and the increasing involvement of other local political players. Will we end up with two judicial systems and two types of police? From the local through to the international level there is a need to reconstruct our institutions according to this paradigm.

Terrorism

Terrorism is the new major face of the planet's anxiety. Though states no longer declare war, they declare war on terrorism. A few years ago it was drugs. It is true that the technical capabilities of mass destruction have become such that the destruction wreaked by terrorism can be equivalent to that of an army campaign.

---

1. Committee of Ministers Recommendation No. R (2001)11 concerning guiding principles on the fight against organised crime (19 September 2001), Council of Europe .
2. *Europol annual report 2001*, 7267/01 Europol 23.
3. *Local approach of organised crime* (based on Safety and Democracy Colloquy) European Forum for Urban Security, Paris, 2000.

Terrorism lives at the corner of our street, it is among us, with us. Combating it raises the problem of our social organisation. The freedoms we have given ourselves and defend are also those that can help the terrorist to act. This therefore raises the question of the future of our freedoms and the individual rights which form the basis of our democracies.

Are we prepared to accept restrictions? In a document adopted by the Committee of Ministers on the fight against terrorism, states are given the possibility of exemption from certain obligations enshrined in international treaties:

> When the fight against terrorism takes place in a situation of war or public emergency which threatens the life of the nation, a State may adopt measures temporarily derogating from certain obligations ensuing from the international instruments of protection of human rights, to the extent strictly required by the exigencies of the situation, as well as within the limits and under the conditions fixed by international law. The State must notify the competent authorities of the adoption of such measures in accordance with the relevant international instruments.[1]

The Council considered that, in view of its fundamental mission, it had a duty to recall that "terrorism seriously jeopardises human rights, threatens democracy, and aims notably to destabilise legitimately constituted governments and to undermine pluralistic civil society".

The Council of Europe teaches a lesson of optimism by recalling that it is "it is not only possible, but also absolutely necessary, to fight terrorism while respecting human rights, the rule of law and, where applicable, international humanitarian law". Is this not an exercise intrinsically linked to the relative weakness of the democratic state?

The other danger of terrorism is that it leaves exceptional provisions in our legislation that gradually come to be used to deal with other types of violence and crime. While it may be possible to accept anonymous testimony in proceedings concerning terrorism and organised crime, it is surprising to find such measures being used to combat neighbourhood crime on the grounds that the community connections between offender and victim give rise to fears that pressure may be exerted. This is the case in the United Kingdom, where a "Crimestoppers trust" programme is being developed, and in France with the Act of July 2002.

The Council of Europe has stipulated that exemptions from international conventions should be temporary: "The circumstances which led to the adoption of such derogations need to be reassessed on a regular basis with the purpose of lifting these derogations as soon as these circumstances no longer exist". No such provision has been made with respect to domestic law!

Insecurity

Insecurity or, more exactly, the feeling of insecurity, is prospering. The objective conditions of our immediate security have never been better, but our anxiety is

---

1. *Guidelines of the Committee of Ministers of the Council of Europe on human rights and the fight against terrorism,* Council of Europe Publishing, 2002, XV-p. 12.

intensifying. It feeds upon all the questions about our collective futures and all our fears about our ability to affirm our individualism in an environment we do not control.

Faced with this environment, we adopt contradictory attitudes: we demand the eradication of a number of threats while we accept others that we simply try to reduce. We eliminate violence and crime and reduce tobacco, drugs and pollution. The conceptualisation of risk reduction with the invention of the principle of pre-caution has entered numerous public policies.[1] As an example we need only remember the "mad cow" crisis. What has to be done for it to penetrate the field of crime? Insurance has helped to reduce the harm suffered as a result of crime and ought to have encouraged us to adopt the approach of risk reduction with respect to crime.

Facts and figures are not alone in fuelling insecurity. Other people's insecurity has become our own: fear is everywhere, even in the safest places. Insecurity is in our heads and is increasingly governing our behaviour.

Violence and its territories

For a long time the world was binary, divided into two camps, each convinced that it embodied all virtues and had to combat the malevolent influence of the other. For communist regimes, crime, drugs and prostitution reflected a system that exploited individuals, subjecting them to an implacable economic logic. If communism were to experience such phenomena it would only be on a temporary basis. The world has become complex; alliances and models are being sought.

Violence in states

The collapse of the communist empires has left the world in a state of contradictions. These are fuelled as much by social and economic modernisation and the reconstruction or break-up of states as a result of the reawakening of ethnic groups and peoples as by the questioning of the distinctions between "public" and "private", "internal" and "external".

There is much talk of the disappearance of states to the benefit of globalisation or political accords. What is tending to disappear is perhaps less states themselves than their monopoly of violence. The confrontation of the United States with the al-Qaeda terrorist network is representative of this displacement of the control of violence towards its uncontrolled dissemination. The transition to democracy in eastern Europe has taken place at the price of an upsurge of civil and political violence, while in the past some Latin American and African countries emerging from periods of dictatorship erupted into civil war. There is no civil war in eastern Europe, but there is a huge rise in crime and in the feeling of insecurity. These countries have gone from totalitarian violence to low-level terrorist violence and infrequent, limited political violence; but they have also acquired a pathological

---

1. Cities such as Ljubljana (Slovenia) have appointed a risk manager responsible for civil protection and crime issues.

fear of insecurity, private, targeted violence and above all institutionalised violence in the ways the police, the army and prisons operate.

The state is confronted with private groups which have strategies to compete for control of certain activities but do not seek to overturn the government. This organised crime goes hand in hand with the internationalisation of the economic arena and is becoming established in Europe, seeking alliances with the older criminal groups in the west or fighting them. Its ability to adapt is impressive, using the most modern and the oldest methods simultaneously.

Modes of urbanisation and the accentuation of social inequalities, combined with spatial segregation, provide potential for the development of territorialised collective violence. But forms of violence find expression indiscriminately in unexpected places and public spaces. The violence that now accompanies certain sports and events has become endemic. Places we once thought sheltered from violence, such as schools, have been caught up in the whirlwind.

Violence in cities

Every city having faced any of the following knows it cannot simply call upon the public authority responsible for public safety:

– an outbreak of violence;

– the community divided into hostile closed territories;

– not enough places in school and/or parents refusing to enrol their children in school;

– too many young people on the job market;

– demands for security, more police, more severe punishment are recurrent themes of public debate;

– a fast growing supply of security equipment and services.

It must, with other levels of government and other partners, analyse and perhaps adapt its development, movements, spaces and services to its inhabitants.

The many meetings organised by the European Forum for Urban Security (EFUS) between European cities over the last ten years also show that our categories of representations of violence have changed. The definition both politicians and lawyers give of violence does not completely take into account the forms of violence experienced on a daily basis. A study conducted by the European forum in six European cities[1] showed the nature of violence to be very varied and particular to each city according to its culture and the origin of its inhabitants. The cities of northern Europe are more susceptible to group phenomena and the regular con-

---

1. Liverpool (United Kingdom), Portsmouth (United Kingdom), Antwerp (Belgium), Modena (Italy), L'Hospitalet (Spain), Alcobendas (Spain), Frankfurt (Germany), Kiel (Germany), Erfurt (Germany), Cascais (Portugal); research for the study "Violences urbaines en Europe, police de proximité en Europe", 2000, was conducted by the Institut des hautes études de la sécurité intérieur, Paris.

frontations they engender, while the cities of southern Europe are more likely to experience problems engendered by drugs and alcohol.

Petty acts previously perceived as breaches of customary codes – relating to social or cultural positions, or public spaces – are now coming into the category of violence. Such a shift takes place when the individual or collective ability to correct the behaviour, the breach of custom, is lost. Such impotence is seen as established violence. Such lack of assurance with respect to a situation has become everyday fact for the citizens of European cities. No longer saying anything to the young man who puts his feet on the seat of the train or to noisy neighbours plunges us into endured violence which may be transformed into open violence. Little by little, police and judicial authorities are called upon to deal with this type of incident and enjoined ever more curtly to take action. It is useless to point out that, without mentioning the increased workload such cases represent, these institutions are not equipped to intervene in such matters, and what is more, may have a negative effect on their outcome. A number of studies show that most of the incidents reported to the police are not of a criminal nature and should be the responsibility of other services (social, health, education, housing, and so forth).

This type of urban violence is not listed in the statistics. The gravity of the offences established by criminal law no longer corresponds to the reality of violence in cities. Surveys on insecurity always show that people do not perceive hold-ups as a factor in insecurity.

There is no longer any sanctuary from this many-faced violence. It is among us; it is a continuum of our lives, thoughts and modes of action.

Visible and invisible violence

Why are some forms of violence talked about and others not? Some forms of violence are emerging, others disappearing.

Acknowledged violence

Over the last twenty years we have become aware of violence against women; violence in the family, the violence of partners in social and working life. All the inequalities that have existed and been described for centuries but accepted (as a reality?) by everyone have become unacceptable and are now denounced as violence. The consensus was shattered by the mobilisation of women, but also by the at least tacit agreement of men. This "revelation" has been accompanied by a questioning of the social and economic status of women. What is more, the representation of this type of violence – to whose dissemination numerous international conferences have greatly contributed[1] – has appeared in a similar fashion on the international arena. The revelation of sexual violence against children is taking longer to reach the same worldwide scale.

---

1. Declaration and Platform for Action adopted at the 4th World Conference on Women in Beijing in 1995, United Nations.

"Localised" violence

Other manifestations are more confined to certain regions or countries. They may be more a matter of the culture or economic and social situation of particular countries. Although female excision is mentioned in United Nations documents, it remains a regional problem, some regions strongly resisting calls to put an end to it.

One of the main obstacles to the signing of the United Nations Convention on the Rights of the Child by some countries was the right for adults to inflict corporal punishment on children. Was it an essential component of upbringing, a right or ill-treatment? This question arises frequently in the western European institutions concerned with children at risk who are confronted with parents from African or Arab cultures claiming the right to punish. The European Court of Human Rights dealt with the question in a 1982 judgment which led to corporal punishment being prohibited in all public and private schools in the United Kingdom.

"Uncertain violence"

Other violence-related issues are about to emerge, although it is still unclear which spheres they belong to. For example, listening to public debate, there seems to be uncertainty as to the priorities with respect to trafficking in human beings: is it more important to destroy the criminal organisations behind the trafficking or to take into account the violence of which the women and young people involved are victims? There are two opposing conceptions: one that regards prostitution as a reality and seeks to regulate the conditions in which the profession is conducted, free of all forms of violence, and another that considers violence inherent to the work and that no measure will ever do anything to reduce it. The globalisation of markets, the establishment of channels from the countries of eastern Europe and the circulation of prostitutes between European cities have taken this type of crime into the sphere of organised crime. Is it condemned because it is organised or because it is violent?

Yet another example is violence on the roads. Many European countries do not have well-developed preventive and punitive policies on violence on the roads. It is not a priority for the European Union, in particular for its crime prevention pro-gramme. Yet the number of deaths, particularly of young people, in road accidents in Europe is considerable. Nearly 40% of victims are in the 14-25 age group. When one looks at national reports on crime, one sees that road crime is not regarded as an important form of violence. The World Health Organisation classi-fies this type of injury unintentional. Some countries have reclassified such behaviour in the category of intentional acts and therefore as violence. Should not the freedom of movement, which is one of the foundations on which Europe is being built, be accompanied by a common interest in such violence? Is it right that my chances of being killed or wounded should vary according to the European country through which I am travelling? In 2001, the Mans report of the Congress of Local and Regional Authorities of Europe (CLRAE) introduced the car into the scope of urban crime prevention after a resolution adopted at the Szczecin Conference had adopted the principle of safe urban travel.

A conjunction of interests is better than no interest at all. These examples show that our indignation still varies and differs in degree on the international scale of gravity, as our international comparisons demonstrate.

Forgotten violence

While we are becoming aware of some types of violence, others are tending to disappear. For example, violence in the workplace is gradually being revealed. This essentially covers violence between workers and violence by superiors against inferiors in the division of labour.[1] It is fortunate that this type of violence, which we now realise is extraordinarily widespread, is coming to light, but at the same time one notes that a few years ago talking about violence at work meant talking about violence against workers because of their working conditions, wages and precarious status as employees, unilateral disciplinary power and the frequency of industrial accidents. It would seem that, under the pressure of economic recession and global competition in recent years, these issues have become secondary or at least are no longer perceived as violence. Hence, in particular, the difficulty the international community is having in dealing with the issue of child labour in developing countries, an issue that gives rise to debate focusing more on obstacles to development and the necessary evil to be tolerated for the sake of a better future. Child labour has not entered the category of unacceptable forms of violence.

Juvenile violence

The association of young people and violence has become an unavoidable theme in international debate. In addition to the question as to whether such violence has increased dramatically, one is struck by the fact that the issue is above all of concern to European countries with ageing populations.

Young people form the largest category of victims of violence. According to the *World report on violence and health* published in October 2002 by the World Health Organisation, more than 36% of deaths were the result of acts of violence affecting young people in the 10-29 age group. The highest risks of being the victim of all forms of violence are concentrated in this age group. Such violence may be perpetrated by gangs, young people in the street or at school. Involvement in physical confrontations and the use of weapons are the most frequent risks.

A survey conducted by the European Forum for Urban Security on juvenile justice in 2000[2] found that the proportion of total crime for which minors were responsible was not rising and was even falling, but that all the officials questioned were concerned about forms of violence involving juveniles. No one hid their concern

---

1. Two per cent of workers in the EU are the victims of physical violence by their colleagues; 4% are victims of persons from outside the company; 2% are subjected to sexual harassment; 9% are subjected to psychological harassment. This results in high levels of absenteeism and rates of depression. Source: European Foundation for the Improvement of Living and Working Conditions, December 2000.
2. *Les justices des mineurs en Europe,* Ministère de la Justice , France, 2000.

about the apparent inadequacy of the ways in which judicial systems were currently responding. Many countries have in recent years amended legislation on procedure and the authorities responsible for juveniles. Legal changes are also taking place in a public climate that reflects the deep concern of citizens.

European politicians show great confusion about the age of criminal liability and the minimum age at which imprisonment should be authorised. There are great differences in Europe in this respect. The age of criminal liability is 16 in Portugal and Lithuania, 15 in Denmark, Sweden, Finland and Slovak Republic, and 14 in Germany, Austria, Spain, Italy and Romania; it is 7 in Greece and Ireland and 10 in the United Kingdom and France. It is therefore strange to observe that the majority of European countries have set the same age of civil majority (18), in other words, they consider that young persons under 18 may not marry without consent, take out a bank loan or start a company, but differ on the question of their liability to criminal prosecution.[1] These differences show the extent to which this is a political issue.

The European forum survey also showed that most of the changes about to be introduced in countries tend to make systems more severe. Imprisonment and renewed interest in custodial reformatory institutions for young offenders are the flagships of the reconstruction of the criminal law on juveniles under way in most European countries. Italy has set up reception centres to avoid minors coming into contact with the prison population. They are establishments to which minors may be sent for a maximum of four days before appearing in court; the court may of course extend the period. The Swedish Act of 1 January 1999 introduced custodial centres to replace prison where young people may stay for up to four years and be gradually integrated into local society. Portugal has introduced a similar system, as has France, which already has custodial institutions for young offenders. The United Kingdom has set up an intensive programme[2] to take charge of the 2 500 young people found guilty of one quarter of offences. This programme takes charge of the young people around the clock.

What does all this mean? That the minors of the 21st century are harder than those of the 20th, that the problems have worsened, that forms of violence have become more radical? All criminologists reject these conclusions. The first report[3] in Germany on crime and crime control, drafted by ten of the most eminent German criminologists, concluded that, while some forms of violence have emerged, they are not of a kind that should lead to changes in legislation, in particular to a lowering of the age of criminal liability or the more frequent imposition of custodial sentences.

---

1. Lode Walgrave and Jill Mehl, eds., *Confronting youth in Europe: juvenile crime and juvenile justice,* Institute of Local Government Studies, Denmark, August 1998.
2. "Intensive supervision and surveillance" programme.
3. *First periodical report on crime and crime control in Germany,* Federal Ministry of the Interior and Ministry of Justice, Berlin, July 2001.

The same report quotes a survey conducted by the Criminological Research Institute of Lower Saxony for the years 1998-2000: more than 80% of offences were not reported to the police, although the rate had improved, but above all young people were the principal victims of other young people. Another survey of the schools of five German cities conducted in 2000 found that 9% of young people had been sexually abused, 13% were subjected to severe forms of punishments and that young immigrants were three times more likely to be victims. While two-thirds of young people had committed an offence in the previous year, only 3% of offences were thefts. This shows that many young people have a relationship with violence and delinquency but that this is only a passing phase.

In the history of criminal institutions, the progress made was to introduce rules creating exceptions for juveniles. Does this have to be called into question at the risk of forgetting the social and family origins of the behaviour of some young people?

We should remain calm but our calm should not blind us to the new phenomena involving young people as authors or victims. The fact that young people from Africa and eastern Europe roam around many cities in southern Europe worries the authorities of those cities a great deal. The means – including the educational means – available for dealing with young people without papers who have decided to return to their countries only when they have made a success of things are limited and made more difficult by linguistic problems. Some young people are taken charge of by adults who force them to beg, prostitute themselves or steal. Such problems, which are of great significance neither in terms of the numbers involved nor of their impact on crime, require a transnational approach that will revise modes of action. Co-operation between professionals in different countries is essential and a common reference framework of preventive methods needs to be drawn up.

Media globalisation of violence

The Internet and the hundreds of television channels now in existence have globalised the representation of violence. We cannot escape our neighbour's violence. The antipodes are now part of our immediate environment. From hidden violence, the representation of which was censored, we have moved into a world of permanent violence.

Death without taboo

The change can be measured through the history of the representation of the results of death, violent death in particular. The representation of death, of massacred corpses, was for a long time taboo and there was implicit agreement not to show it. Until the second world war, the taboo was generally respected. The representation of nazi camps and mass graves broke the taboo. This was done with the aim of showing how legitimate the war had been and in the hope that such political theories would never regain popularity. From that time on, the taboo was gradually lifted and the representation of death was often used in a political battle which little by little came to understand the importance of images. Interpersonal violence also gradually found expression in images.

The taboo suddenly re-emerged on 11 September 2001 when the American authorities obtained the agreement of the press not to film the bodies. Some people rightly said that the prohibition could also be applied to other scenes of horror and that propriety should be observed with respect to all deaths.

This perhaps provides international institutions with the opportunity to reflect upon the constant representation of the worst atrocities and perhaps on the way such morbid interest could be controlled. While the representation of dead bodies has been used to provoke reactions of indignation of the "never again" variety, indignation is rare and the images are perhaps losing their power. Such reflection would certainly make it possible to approach the issue of the representation of violence in the media more satisfactorily.

Virtual violence

For a number of years the media have felt a desperate need for reality and fiction to resemble each other more closely. The representation of crime on television has always been a prime source of romantic inspiration. Every country has cult police series in which the scenarios oppose police forces and the forces of darkness constantly threatening the balance of our lives and cities. The content of such series has disseminated a way of thinking that is American in inspiration. Crime and its modes of expression have become American, particularly in the frequent use of firearms, the ways in which the police intervene and court proceedings. Some lawyers have compared legislative development in Europe with the model offered in media representations. The questioning of suspects conducted by some European police forces is a carbon copy of that of their American colleagues. These changes in intervention techniques do not seem to be the result of a change in European crime patterns or more dangerous behaviour on the part of offenders.

To supplement fictional series, which are perhaps running out of steam, television has given itself the task of hunting down the perpetrators of real crimes. Live filming of arrests, filming tailing and other police techniques, filming confessions, filming trials, conducting live investigations or re-enacting them, are all types of "reality shows" that often take great liberties with individual rights.

Do the media encourage crime?

Do the media influence the commission of offences? Many studies have been undertaken on this subject. Some American and German studies have concluded that they have little such influence. It is difficult to determine whether people who watch a violent film and then imitate it watched it because they were impelled by psychological factors particular to them or if they were "subjugated" by the image. A distinction has to be drawn between the media as conveyor of violence in the world – representations of conflicts, massacres and abductions – and works created in images. Videos seem to be a greater problem, but we do not really know its extent.

The *First periodical report on crime and crime control in Germany,* published in 2001 by the Ministry of Justice and the Ministry of the Interior devotes a great deal of attention to copycat crime. Specialists found that the broadcasting of reports about crimes led young people to imitate them. This was observed with respect to the propagation of some urban riots and, more seriously, with the propagation of racial and anti-Semitic crimes. Copycat offenders are the counterparts of the globalisation of events and the multiplication of images that propel local news items to the headlines of world news. The ambiguity comes from the fact that such images are sometimes broadcast with the intention of condemning the acts committed, particularly in the case of anti-Semitism, but have the opposite effect. The police are familiar with this sort of chain reaction. They see its effects in relation to racist violence against migrants when, for example, acts of aggression in England that receive wide media coverage are reproduced in Germany or, as has happened in France several times, urban violence, such as setting light to cars, has spread to other areas. Similarly, new *modi operandi* of delinquency are transmitted very quickly.

The pornographic economy has taken over the media. The turnover of this industry contributes a great deal to the financing of many media. Access to films raises the problem of the influence such pornography has over children. Experts unanimously agree that it particularly influences young people discovering their own sexuality. But can one go further and say that openly violent behaviour is caused by it? It is possible that sexual behaviour has been transformed – some surveys show that fellatio, the *sine qua non* of pornographic representation, is more frequently practised by adults – but are people led to reproduce masochistic violence and the contempt for women all such films portray? Do we know to what extent the violence and contempt contained in the images children look at will be expressed in their adult lives?

The media against reason

Reality has become one with fiction and this is producing a feeling of danger at every moment of our lives. The exceptional and the serious are becoming ordinary and reality is being reinterpreted by what the image that is given to us conveys. Everything is crime, everything is subject to future disaster. The serenity of debates on insecurity has been shattered. If someone says we run less risk of being murdered on the streets of our cities than we did fifty years ago, their words go unheard; the argument that is 100 000 times more likely to be injured in a road accident is not believed, and anyone who says so may even be suspected of trying to mask the truth. The fact that there is a 1 in 100 million chance of being attacked in the Paris metro carries little weight with American tourists who are convinced it is dangerous. The media are not interested in the fact that we are more likely to suffer violence from our relatives than from strangers. The promoters of prevention policies, that multitude of actions with extraordinarily positive effects, are pushed into the shadows of non-communication. The arguments that can put the objective gravity of the phenomenon into perspective are perceived as a betrayal of the victims and a sign of "softness" on the part of people who enjoy social situations that protect them from danger.

Crusading media

The media are everywhere purveyors of the demand that insecurity should be eradicated absolutely. The 1996 recommendation of the Committee of Ministers of the Council of Europe[1] recalling that the aim of a crime prevention policy is not to eliminate crime but to reduce it have been largely forgotten. The desire for eradication, elimination, absolute cleanness, has found its slogan in the doctrine of "zero tolerance", a moral that is transformed into totalitarianism when it is embodied in social policy or political expression.

In recent years a great many countries have become aware of the scale of the sexual abuse of children and massive awareness campaigns have been launched. These campaigns have on several occasions taken a worrying turn with man hunts, public denunciations and the formation of vigilante groups. Rights and freedoms have been seriously violated. Men and women who have not been convicted of any offence have been subjected to social exclusion, have lost their jobs and their whole families. The history of the appearance of the doctrine of "zero tolerance" is instructive: it was first used to raise awareness of the injustice suffered by women subjected to violence that the police and courts regarded as normal or even treated with scepticism, and has now been extended to cover all offences! The hypocrisy of the slogan and of those who wish to apply it is that it is generally used selectively. The authors of only certain kinds of offences are hounded and it is a particular category of the population that is targeted, namely the homeless, immigrants and young people. Major scandals concerning financial crime enjoy an extraordinary degree of tolerance or even complicity from social and professional elites.

The crisis in the legitimacy of authorities is fuelling this substitution role played by the media. Both police and judiciary are suspected of not doing their jobs with respect to cases involving "important people". The crisis is further fuelled by the revelation of cases of corruption and secret funding involving elected representatives.[2] An international poll of 35 000 people found that 70% of those questioned regarded their elected representatives as corrupt. The percentage rose to 90% in Latin America and the Far East. The corruption of elected representatives is all the more painfully experienced since it often occurs in countries in which the transition to the market economy has resulted in a rise in poverty. The Council of Europe has rightly made the corruption of public officials one of the central parameters of urban insecurity which undermines public confidence in the will and ability of leaders to reduce it.[3]

---

1. Committee of Ministers Recommendation No. R (96) 8 on crime policy in Europe in a time of change, Council of Europe.
2. *Gallup international 50th anniversary survey,* online publication (see: http: www.gallup-international.com/survey1).
3. See *Urban crime prevention – a guide for local authorities,* Council of Europe Publishing, 2002.

II. MEASURING VIOLENCE

Unmeasured violence

What are we talking about when we speak of insecurity and violence in Europe? We have seen the appalling diversity of the interpretation of such notions and the difficulty of reducing insecurity. This is all the more true since what is at issue is not only an objective risk but an irrational, exaggerated perception.

During the period 1960-80, rates of increase in recorded crime were the highest in European history. Current per capita crime rates were reached by the end of that period. However, the question of insecurity interested only a small group of criminologists and professionals and was not a subject of public debate or anxiety in Europe. One of the explanations of this is economic prosperity, not so much because of its high level as because there was sustained growth. Since then we have been in phases of strong growth but accompanied always by anxiety about an uncertain future. We have entered an unstable world in which everything could change at any time.

The construction of measurement

The statistics reflect the activity of police forces rather than actual offending. Variations in the figures are closely dependent on the organisation of police forces and their activity. Because of insurance systems based on reporting to the police, quite high rates are reported for some offences and apparently reflect the actual situation accurately, while reporting rates for other offences are very low.

Some offences may remain largely invisible, such as violence against women which was for a long time a subject of general indifference and accepted by the people concerned. The numerous campaigns conducted in individual countries, the repeated action of international institutions and the mobilisation of women have gradually changed the situation, which is another problem to be borne in mind when analysing the statistics. Can one say that the level of violence against women is constant or actually rising? A few more years of awareness campaigning will be needed before the figure reaches its true level and provides the beginnings of a reply.

Caution is needed when reading the statistics. Specialists consider that a trend describes a situation more reliably than a snapshot. A film is better than a photo. A steady fall in crime over four years is credible; a sharp fall in the incidence of an offence in one year suggests technical problems in data collection or management, rather than an actual fall. Such caution prevailed in the first European report on juvenile violence requested by the Dutch presidency of the European Union in

1998, which found, not an increase in juvenile violence, but greater attention paid to young people by police forces.[1]

Victim surveys

Because of the unreliability of police statistics, victim surveys are conducted with varying frequency in different countries. They are included in annual police statistics in the countries of northern Europe, but are less frequent elsewhere. Most countries use the United Nations victim survey conducted[2] every four years to have a better idea of their national situation. The efforts of the United Nations to publish a sort of world atlas essentially containing the findings of a victim survey in more than 120 countries, the United Nations *Global report on crime and justice*,[3] are to be welcomed, although the comparisons are valid only for comparable regions of the world. While in the first case the victim survey may become a working instrument able to correct punitive and preventive policies, in the second, they are merely reference tools for academics, of little use to operational staff.

A third tool is being developed in the form of self-reported offending surveys which question subjects about the offences they have committed (whether or not they have been the subject of criminal proceedings). Such surveys sometimes target certain categories of the population, young people, for example, in order to find out their relationship with drugs,[4] or prisoners in order to find out the real level of offending. In the latter case, surveys make it easier to determine the level of re-offending and in all cases the ability of the police system to solve cases.

Difficulty of accurately measuring violence

It is difficult to discover what offences are actually being committed at national level and, paradoxically, difficult to discover how much crime there is at local level. The paradox lies in the fact that most efficient insecurity alleviation policies are implemented in cities and that it is extremely difficult to obtain official data on the precise area in which local officials have chosen to act. A comparative study on violence in the cities of Antwerp, Erfurt, Liverpool, Frankfurt, Kiel, Cascais and Portsmouth conducted for the European Forum for Urban Security in 2000[5] found that the cities had provided themselves with specific instruments for measuring violence since they had not found the necessary information in national statistics.

---

1. Christian Pfeiffer, "Trends in juvenile violence in European countries" (Noordwijk Conference) Kriminologisches Forschungsinstitut Niedersachsen, Hanover 1998.
2. Study conducted every four years by the United Nations Interregional Crime and Justice Research Institute with the co-operation of the governments of the Netherlands, the United Kingdom and Northern Ireland.
3. *Global report on crime and justice*, Office for Drug Control and Crime Prevention, United Nations,1999.
4. Survey on self-reported offending conducted in 1995, 1997, and 1999 on 6 000 pupils aged 15 by the National Crime Prevention Council of Stockholm.
5. *Urban violence and community policing in Europe,* European Forum for Urban Security, Paris.

The difficulty is still greater when one tries to establish crime levels at international level. We are in an extraordinary situation in which politicians, professionals and the media talk about organised crime without being able to quote any figures on the actual levels of such crime. No international observatory has been given the task of recording it, so the same case will be counted in each country concerned and arrests in several countries will also be included in national statistics. The international debate is a constant extrapolation from what individuals see in their own countries and what they perceive as the inability of law enforcement agencies to deal with such crime.[1] "Enquiries are complicated, so if the police in my country have detected one case, it means that ninety-nine others have gone undetected!" Such reasoning means there are good times ahead for police officers claiming more funding, politicians making speeches and public opinion getting used to the idea that the people responsible for policies are doing nothing and are incapable of curbing a serious threat that is challenging the laws on which our societies are based.

It is also difficult to compare national crime figures. According to the Secretary General of the United Nations,[2] many countries consider that providing statistics on crime would tarnish their reputation and might discourage investors. Furthermore, cultural differences and differences in perceptions of crime throw doubt on the comparability of some offences at world level. Definitions of offences differ too widely for us to be able to compare Luxembourg with Indonesia. In other words, some community of civilisation or at least knowledge of the differences is needed if analyses are to be made. If I know that killing a dog is not murder in the country to which I wish to compare my own, I can start to make a comparison. This is why sharing common values gives hope that Europe might be able to provide itself with a credible instrument of comparison.

The need for a European observatory

It is not a question of discovering whether the incidence of violence has changed, whether the atrocious has become more ferocious and commonplace, whether violence has increased in volume – this would be like trying to count the grains of sand in a desert. There is no point in saying that we are more secure now than we were in the 18th century when there were no aeroplanes, firearms or televisions and people were drawn and quartered in places of public execution. Horrors continue, including during regional conflicts. Europe learned – without reacting very strongly – that they were even able to erupt in its own territory in the late 20th century.

While the moral principle condemning violence now governs the international community, when applied to particular situations we can see that it suffers from many exceptions. Nor is there any need to keep the table of the representation and hierarchy of violence up to date, deliver labels of democracy or introduce a

---

1. We should stress the efforts made by the UN Centre for International Crime Prevention in Vienna, which has undertaken a number of studies, in particular on the social and economic costs of crime.
2. "The state of crime and criminal justice worldwide", report by the Secretary General to the 10th United Nations Congress on the Prevention of Crime and Treatment of Offenders, United Nations, April 2000.

standardised international hierarchy. Why one and not the other? In the name of what higher value? There is always something dangerous about a standardised hierarchy in that, historically, it has preceded the unleashing of crusades to impose it.

Setting priorities for particular regions and countries may encourage internal changes in perception and therefore of representation. In this dialogue of violence and reason, the constantly unravelling of the red string of our fears and anxieties, an inventory must be made of the extraordinary proliferation of the safeguards we have invented to avoid the complete defeat of reason. Explaining the conditions of the emergence of one or other form of violence and the disappearance of another could be included in the work of an observatory which would be especially useful for the internal life of states and, as a consequence, international life.

The wish of the Parliamentary Assembly of the Council of Europe that an observatory on crime and insecurity[1] should be created is extremely apposite in view of the abundance of common legal instruments, definitions, standards and codes of conduct, and, above all, a case-law that is, by its nature, constantly changing and encourages harmonisation. In addition, the stabilisation of the former communist countries, and particularly their criminal justice systems, makes it possible to enter a positive phase of crime-trend analysis in Europe.

European figures on violence

What are the crime trends in Europe?[2]

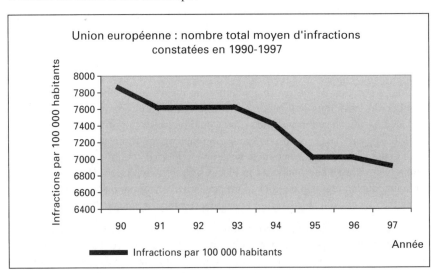

Union européenne : nombre total moyen d'infractions constatées en 1990-1997

Source: United Nations

1. Parliamentary Assembly Recommendation 1531 (2001) on security and crime prevention in cities: setting up a European Observatory, Council of Europe.
2. Crime-trend tables taken from the "Report by the Secretary General of the United Nations to the 10th UN Congress on the Prevention of Crime and Treatment of Offenders", April 2000.

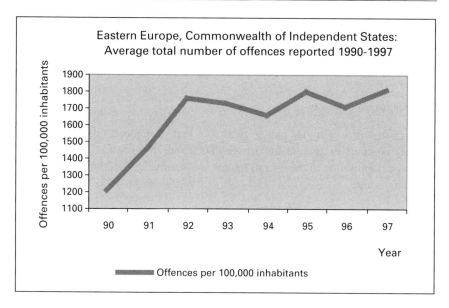

Source: United Nations

The difference between the east and the west

In the years 1990-2000, crime was generally stabilising and even falling, more markedly in the countries of western Europe. The countries emerging from the communist period of course experienced significant rises in their figures. For example, the number of offences rose from 340 to 450 thousand in Hungary, 38 to 67 thousand in Slovenia and 23 to 57 thousand in Estonia.

But how much did crime actually increase, given that the setting-up of a policing system accessible to all naturally increased the number of complaints? The communist countries had for years accustomed their inhabitants to living "without crime", since offences were not recorded, at least officially as socialist well-being could not be disturbed by the existence of such phenomena and victims could hope for neither compensation nor remedy by reporting a wrong. With the opening-up of these countries and political change, the phenomenon began to emerge from the shadows. Moreover, the deterioration of the economic situation and the lack of government favoured the great and speedy rises in crime rates that shook people's convictions and certainties. This, without any doubt, contributed to the problems involved in establishing democratic systems of government in the face of demagogues whose aims were often linked to the interests of organised crime.

At the same time, crime rose from 3.4 to 3.7 million units in France and 4.5 to 5.1 million in the United Kingdom, while it remained stable in Spain (at 1 million), as it did in Sweden, Denmark and Italy, and fell in countries such as Bulgaria, Slovak Republic and Finland. Victim surveys show that two-thirds of the population of Europe will be victims of crime in the next six years and that 1 person in 5 will be the victim of a serious act (particularly aggression).

It is misleading to measure all crime in a single indicator, since the result is to add up turnips and carrots. Some offences are less tolerable for people than others, or more serious for the country. Unfortunately, cases of organised crime are buried in this type of measurement.

Property versus persons

Changes in terms of trends enable us to say that, in general, offences against property continue to account for between 60% and 75% of total crime and that falls in or stabilisation of the overall figures are mainly the result of the decline in this main group.

Offences against property are falling because of the growth of private property protection systems and also because of economic development and rising incomes. Germany experienced a significant fall of 60% in car thefts between 1993 and 1999. This trend can also be confirmed *a contrario* by the higher proportion of offences against property in the countries of eastern Europe.

For example, Ukraine experienced an appreciable fall in crime between 1996 and 2000, but offences against property rose by more than ten points. Armenia experienced a similar increase in offences against property (+11). Estonia has seen an increase in theft of more than 70%. These increases go hand in hand with an "economic take-off" that is not accompanied by property protection equivalent to that in western Europe. It can also be noted that, the closer one moves west, the more crime curves tend to resemble those of the countries of western Europe.

In western Europe, falls in offences against property are greater than increases in offences against persons. In international comparisons[1] the latter include attacks against the person, armed attacks and sex crimes. They are increasing, and very seriously so, in most countries. For example, between 1996 and 2000, attacks against the person rose by 38% in Spain, 13% in Sweden, 17% in Denmark, 20% in Italy and Slovak Republic and 11% in Finland, while Finland, along with Ireland, experienced the greatest fall in crime in the decade concerned. We are indeed, therefore, faced with a problem of violence, but violence which is, despite everything, limited to a certain degree of gravity.

Murder rates stable

The number of murders is astonishingly stable: the thirty-nine European countries composing a panel record a slight fall (of one point) in the murder rate and the rate is even falling sharply in most European countries, so much so that the few countries where the indicator rose between 1996 and 2000 can be quoted: England,

---

1. Gordon Barclay and Cynthia Tavares, "International comparisons of criminal justice statistics 2000", UK Home Office Bulletin.

Belgium, Ireland, Norway, Portugal, Slovak Republic and Spain, though no explanation can be offered as to the cause of these increases, some of which are significant, such as Spain (+24%) and Belgium (+34%), while England, which has a relatively low per capita murder rate, has experienced a significant fall in overall crime and one of the lowest increases in the violence indicator in Europe.

Murder is one of the indicators of urban violence. The two countries that stand out significantly on the European scene are the Russian Federation and Estonia, with 20 and 11 murders per 100 000 inhabitants respectively, while the European average is 1.7 (0.8 in Luxembourg)! The rate in Berlin is 2.5, as against 1.2 in Germany as a whole, while it is 9.7 in Vilnius, 5.3 in Warsaw, 3.5 in Bratislava and 3 in Stockholm. Moscow is the murder capital of Europe with a rate of 18.2, but falls far short of Washington, which has 46 murders per 100 000 inhabitants. In order to define more precisely any failings of crime reduction policies in European cities we need to know more about the type of murders and the degree of control of murders in the short or medium term. It is easier to lower the rate of murders proactively if the culprits are leaders of organised crime than if the rate depends on alcohol consumption on Saturday nights, the reduction of which requires lengthy prevention campaigns. The mayor of Bogotá in Colombia has managed to reduce the (very high) number of murders through tight control of the distribution of drink in the city. Possible measures with respect to murder show that violence is not inevitable, and European cities should see themselves as very active agents of crime reduction policies.

Armed violence

There is no doubt that increases in murder rates (the overall average is relatively low compared to the United States, where it is 5.9) can be linked to the civilisation of firearms.[1] Murder rates in the world are automatically correlated with rates of possession of firearms (most often used in family disputes). The distribution of firearms and the ease of obtaining them are risk factors of violence. It is regrettable that international institutions have not taken up this issue, which is also connected to the issue of private police forces, and recommended harmonised legislation in Europe. Legislation restricting the possession and purchase of firearms should be included as indicators of democracy required of some countries seeking to join international organisations.

Violence and drugs

This problem is difficult to analyse and has been exploited in political debate and calls for mobilisation and a war against drugs which are unlikely to move citizens' attitudes on the subject forward.

---

1. Kristina Kangerspunta, *Profiles of criminal justice systems in Europe and North America (90-98)*, European Institute for Crime Prevention and Control, Helsinki, 2000.

Europe is divided between the adoption of a risk reduction policy and the adoption of a radical policy to eliminate drugs by punishing both use and trafficking. The cities and countries of Europe are divided between the two concepts. It is interesting to note the contradictions in this regard within a single country between central and city levels. Following a number of meetings of the cities of Belgium, France, the Netherlands and Germany, the members of the European forum network noted the similarity of police and prosecution practices.[1] In fact, if one looks at the measures European cities are implementing to deal with the problem, one sees they are everywhere dominated by a health approach. The health approach to drug use prevails over the purely criminal approach. The difference lies in the role the criminal justice system plays in access to health and social measures.

The relationship between drugs and violence/crime is expressed in three ways:

– crime linked to trafficking and the other offences connected with the circulation of drugs and money. The analytical problem is the threshold above which the category known as trafficking begins, which is linked in our minds with the question of organised crime or serious crime. We have seen that Europol has abandoned the category of organised crime to take account only of serious crime, which makes it possible to combine several indicators;

– trafficking, which is very common in some neighbourhoods of European cities, organises groups and age groups into the stages of the circulation of the goods (lookout, delivery, etc.) so well that enforcement involves both sophisticated police investigation methods and effective street prevention. Similarly, violence that takes collective forms is often the result of defending a territory against other groups;

– is there a type of violence that can be attributed to drug use? Some crime surveys have concluded that *a modus operandi* may be aggravated by drug-taking, especially with respect to attacks and bloody crimes, but no correlation has been clearly established; nor has it been established that some substances are likely to generate "greater" violence than others.

The survey conducted for the third time by the Council of Europe's Group of Experts in Epidemiology of Drug Problems[2] on a sample of some forty cities enables us to follow changes in trends in drug use and the reactions of criminal justice systems in European countries.

---

1. *Drug-related crossborder traffic patterns,* European Forum for Urban Security, Paris, February 1998.
2. Ruud Bless (with contributions by Uwe Kemmesies and Steven Diemel) *3rd Multi-city study: drug use trends in European cities in the 1990s,* Council of Europe Publishing, 2000.

The trend we should note first is the ten- or fifteen-year delay in the appearance of drugs in the eastern Europe, though the gap closed in the 1990s.

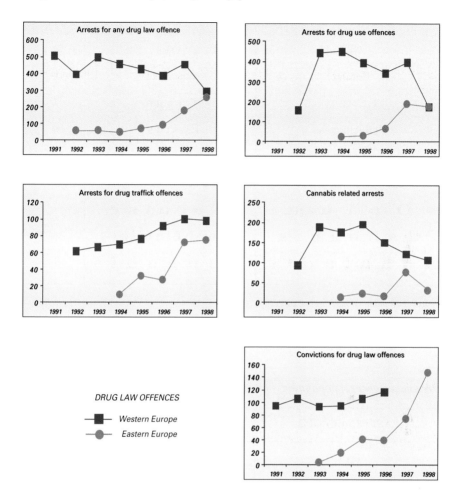

Source: Pompidou Group, Council of Europe

It can be seen how action – very proactive action – by the criminal justice system in the two parts of Europe is tending to be harmonised. The more proactive the police, the more the statistics record increased activity. This increase says little about the actual situation with respect to drugs. The figures probably represent a degree of "lassitude" by the system and could be interpreted as a demand technicians are addressing to politicians to review legislation on the subject.

Analysis at European level of the substances used shows the same growing similarity, though with some differences for heroin and cocaine.

Prevalence general population – early 1990s

EASTERN EUROPE	WESTERN EUROPE	Rank order
Crack	Crack	9
Cocaine	Inhalants	8
Ecstasy	Opium	7
Hallucinogens	Ecstasy	6
Amphetamines	Hallucinogens	5
Heroin	**Heroin**	4
Opium	**Cocaine**	3
Cannabis	**Amphetamines**	2
Inhalants	**Cannabis**	1

Source: Pompidou Group, Council of Europe

Prevalence general population – late 1990s

EASTERN EUROPE	WESTERN EUROPE	Rank order
Crack	Crack	9
Opium	Inhalants	8
Cocaine	Opium	7
Hallucinogens	Heroin	6
Inhalants	Hallucinogens	5
Ecstasy	**Amphetamines**	4
Amphetamines	**Ecstasy**	3
Heroin	**Cocaine**	2
Cannabis	**Cannabis**	1

Source: Pompidou Group, Council of Europe

The promoters of the expert group felt the need to make their observations on the basis of cities since they saw that the market of users and therefore of suppliers had to be concentrated in cities. Furthermore, cities make it easier to specify the size of the populations studied because of the existence of more developed social and health facilities. The table below shows the very worrying gap between the number of drug users and the number of requests for treatment. We leave a large number of problem people in our streets who are likely to fuel a cycle of violence.

Estimate of problem drug use and assumed proposition in treatment, 1997 to 1999

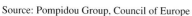

Source: Pompidou Group, Council of Europe

The Council of Europe's Pompidou Group is working with a network of experts in the forty-two cities in the sample. They were asked to give a prognosis of the changes in the problem and the scale of the expected reaction by the authorities. Their opinions are very pessimistic and show a great contrast between eastern and western Europe.

General developments in the 1990s *(n=number of different cities mentioned)*	Responses relating to:	
	EASTERN EUROPE	**WESTERN EUROPE**
Increasing drug problems; situation out of intervention control or developing out of control (n=12)	19	6
Increasing drug problems; low level of control or no longer matched by intervention control (n=13)	20	8
Increasing drug problems; situation remains largely under intervention control (n=15)	1	32
Decreasing drug problems (n=8)	–	15
No (serious) drug problems yet (n=7)	8	4

Source: Pompidou Group, Council of Europe

The drug situation in the cities of western Europe is perceived as being largely under control by health authorities, police forces and judicial systems, and the scale of the problem is seen as in decline. Conversely, the situation in east European cities is seen as being largely out of control with an intensification of the drug problem.

III. INSTITUTIONAL RESPONSES TO VIOLENCE

Attempting to modernise responses to violence

The transformation of violence and the fact that security issues are headline news have profoundly changed national and international responses to violence. There has been considerable change in the institutions involved in these responses, particularly the renewal of the legal arsenal. New actors have arrived on the scene, particularly the private security sector, which is gaining power in many countries, while others are trying to keep it in check through charters, conventions and controls.

The private security sector

No country foresaw that the multiform demand for security would result in such a massive growth in the private security market. In 1987, the Committee of Ministers of the Council of Europe recognised the role of the private surveillance and security sector when it expressed concern that its activities should not hamper the police or threaten individual freedom or public order. It recommended that the activities of such companies should be regulated and positive relations encouraged between police and private sector.[1] Two recent Council of Europe conferences have again emphasised this concern by stressing, in 2001, the need to "ensure ... standards of safety and security, whenever security is handled by the private sector", while, in 2002, "concern was raised about the growing phenomenon of public security provided through private companies. Regulation on a European level of this important and growing sector was called for.[2]

There are risks involved in the development of private security. First, it presents a major problem with respect to the control of public spaces and spaces open to the public. Private security services in such spaces may implement standards different from those of the public sector. The second risk is the production of inegalitarian public spaces. Privately managed spaces certainly enjoy a higher immediate quality of security than those managed by the public sector, but at what price? The division of urban space? This is a major risk for the socio-economic balance of cities. Last, the private sector pressure has contributed to transfers of the services of the criminal justice system. The transfer of prisoners, the guarding of courts, the management of statistics systems and case-law databases are just some of these transfers, not to mention the building and running of prisons. The limitations of such transfers are now clear. Competition to offer the lowest price may have

---

1. Committee of Ministers' Recommendation No. R(87)19 on the organisation of crime prevention, Council of Europe.
2. CLRAE conference in Enschede, Netherlands 20-22 September 2001, multilateral conference in Vilnius, 21-22 March 2002, Council of Europe.

disastrous consequences for the quality of the service. Staff are under-trained, procedures are subject to cuts that undermine the objectives of security. The re-nationalisation of American airport security after 11 September has without any doubt put a permanent brake on the involvement of the private sector in a number of the functions of the criminal justice system.

Partnerships

Modernisation is also taking place through the arrival on the scene of partners taking charge of the various components of security. The police are working with the institutions concerned with "problem areas" and "problem situations". Thus, sectors such as education, culture, training, sports bodies and facilities open to the public are now taking part in the definition and implementation of actions, just as the implementation of actions particular to criminal justice are now using external partners to ensure their success. Sentences served in the community require the participation of people who are responsible for the success of the offender's reintegration. In the mind of the authorities, these changes are motivated as much by the search for savings and a recognition of the inability of the police to deal with problems as by a genuine conviction as to the effectiveness of the policy.

Local elected representatives have also come into the picture. Whatever their administrative, legal or financial jurisdiction, the public have turned to them – since they have no one to turn to in the judicial system or the police – and are implicating and putting pressure on them. Elected representatives are being asked to provide an explanation for the security situation and are accordingly presenting themselves as partners of the criminal justice system and gradually contributing to the invention of the management of security issues at local level.

Costly modernisation

Partial budgetary studies show that budgets allocated to security, including private security, account for between 1.5 and 2.5% of GNP. In the five countries studied (Belgium, France, the Netherlands, Portugal and the United Kingdom), security budgets have increased more than any others. This increase is remedying the inadequacy of existing facilities and enabling police forces to increase the number of officers.

France plans to invest almost 10 billion euros in its criminal justice system between 2002 and 2007, of which 7 billion are to be spent on the police. The United Kingdom plans to spend an additional £3 billion between 2002 and 2006 and recruit 10 000 more police officers. The National Prevention Council of Canada estimates the cost of services to combat crime at $CAD10 billion. These budget increases are for the most part invested in quantity, little being allocated to improving the quality of processes and decisions.

European police forces

Snapping their fingers at our different forms of legal organisation and the relatively well-targeted responsibilities of the police, European citizens report to the police problems over which they have no jurisdiction. At the same time, police management systems take very little account of this situation except by trying to eliminate it as an unproductive, unmeasurable element that should be dealt with by other agencies. Yet such requests of the police reflect people's everyday lives; does not their feeling of insecurity and dissatisfaction with the police come from the fact that when they find no response to their minor problems, they have no reason to believe there will be a response to more serious situations?

Some police forces understand this and take everyday problems into consideration. Spain, for example, has developed a welcoming, respectful police force. This is definitely, however, the lowest common denominator of European police forces. The highest common denominator is the search for visible presence, at the price of increasing the number of police.

The organisation charts of police forces are astonishingly similar, though this does not exclude widely differing situations on the ground.

Varying levels of policing

Comparison of police forces in the European Union by country, area and population[1]

Country	Area km²	Population	Population/ km²	Number of police	Territory covered by one police officer in km²	Population/ police officer
Germany	357 021	82 141 000	230.0	255 002	1.400	322.1
Austria	83 855	8 094 000	96.5	29 205	2.870	277.1
Belgium	30 519	10 246 000	335.7	34 945	0.873	293.2
Denmark	43 094	5 330 000	123.6	10 259	4.200	519.5
Spain	504 782	39 466 000	78.1	192 000	2.620	205.0
Finland	337 030	5 177 000	15.3	7 960	42.340	650.3
France	547 030	59 353 000	108.5	229 715	2.380	258.3
Greece	131 940	10 596 000	80.3	-	-	–
Netherlands	41 532	15 921 000	383.3	40 000	1.030	398.0
Ireland	70 282	3 795 000	53.9	11 235	6.250	337.7
Italy	301 230	57 820 000	191.9	228 000	1.320	253.5
Luxembourg	2 587	433 000	169.3	1 090	2.370	401.8
Portugal	91 906	9 988 500	108.7	45 923	2.000	217.7
Sweden	449 964	8 866 000	19.7	16 500	27.270	537.3
United Kingdom	151 207	52 260 902	345.6	123 841	1.220	422.0

Source: *Diario da Assembleia da Republica (2001)*, Portuguese Ministry of the Interior

---

1. Table taken from the *Diario da assembleia da Republica 2001*, p. 11 (editor's translation). The extremely unusual work of the drafters of the report in placing the Portuguese police in a European context should be noted.

The following partial data for the countries of eastern Europe which could be added to the table:[1] Romania: 210, Slovak Republic 390, Lithuania, 475.

A number of comments need to be made about these data.

First, police numbers vary considerably. All countries have police recruitment programmes but it is unlikely that they will change European rankings significantly over the next ten years. The variation is closely linked to the political history of countries and to their administrative and political organisation.

Also, one is tempted to say that police numbers are not connected with crime. Most southern European countries have very high levels of policing although they have some of the lowest crime rates. France, Spain, Portugal and Italy have 1 police officer per 200 to 260 inhabitants. The type of political system that once existed may explain the high level of policing in some countries; in others, high levels of policing may be a function of the imperatives of internal politics and the existence of civilian police and military police forces.

The perspective (and the ranking of countries) changes if a police/area ratio is introduced, but such a ratio is not a relevant indicator in overwhelmingly urban societies. The explosive growth of cities has thrown police forces off-balance since they have in many cases maintained territorial strengths based more on area than population. It might be said that the best policing models should now be constructed on the basis of problem situations or problem places, most of which are to be found in urban areas.

In recent years, the sharpest rises in crime have been in the countries with the highest levels of policing. What does this mean? Certainly not that the police are responsible for them, since this would be to admit that the police were the only defence against crime, whereas there is also prevention (it would be interesting in this connection to compare the numbers and distribution of social workers and teachers in the same countries). What can at least be said is that the management of policing does not seem to correspond with the types of problems countries are experiencing.

Despite politicians' promises, the constant increase in levels of policing is not satisfying public demand, a fact expressed in the fairly low indicator of satisfaction of victims who have had contact with the police (50%, and around 30% in the countries of central and eastern Europe, according to the United Nations survey). Police officers are more and more expensive, their training is getting longer and longer, their length of service ever shorter and priority is given to strengthening investigation agencies in order to keep pace with the emergence of new types of crime. So much so that more police officers do not necessarily mean more policing, in other words, a sufficiently flexible response to keep pace with changes in offending and with social movement. Our leaders tend to favour police visibility, but such visibility is not a guarantee of good policing. It is simply a guarantee of the presence of the state with respect to a particular objective, namely order in public spaces.

---

1. There is an urgent need for harmonised indicators of activities of the criminal justice system for all Council of Europe member states. This should be one of the tasks of an European observatory.

The fact that some countries have quite low rates of police officers per inhabitant and, at the same time, crime rates that are falling more sharply, suggests that an examination of the policing models operating in countries should take precedence over a purely quantitative approach.

The beginnings of a European policing model?

While a few years ago the differences between the models were fairly easy to identify, they are becoming less clear, as though the outlines of a common model were beginning to emerge. Decentralised organisation of powers was one distinction; the municipalisation of police forces was the dividing line. Since then, centralised police systems have embarked on intensive decentralisation while, conversely, decentralised systems are forming centralised agencies in order to respond more effectively to new types of crime.

Police doctrine states that the police need to have an assessment of the situation in a neighbourhood or territory. This assessment is constantly updated and should make it possible for the daily work of the police to be directed according to the problems identified. Working on the basis of problem situations and problem places is the organisational paradigm. All European police chiefs want to ensure that the means available to and modes of intervention of police officers are constantly adapted to this imperative and that the police are at the service of this mode of intervention. "Community policing", *police de proximité and bürgernahe Polizeiarbeit* have become the organisational slogans of European police forces.

This doctrine also has the advantage of resituating the police in such a way that they are open to the population and their problems. Such openness is not only needed when there are problems and crises, and when crimes are committed, but above all before any of this happens. Preventing crises and offences and strengthening defences against potential crime is the other major aspect of their work that complements the first. British police have a duty to prevent and reduce crime and provide a high quality service to victims and witnesses;[1] German law makes prevention the primary mission of the police.

Partnership is the watchword for all European police forces.[2] Working on prevention and including the factors that cause crime are leading the police to work with a whole range of partners in the public and private sectors. The French police have to be present on local prevention councils, the Dutch police have to engage in dialogue. Such integration may take place with the police remaining the principal actors in security or accepting that they are in equal partnership with others.

Is there a risk that the police may become more autonomous?

It will be clear that, while all European police forces may embrace these three principles (problem-oriented strategy, openness to the population, partnership),

---

1. The United Kingdom "Justice for all", plan presented by the Home Secretary, the Lord Chancellor and the Attorney General, July 2002.
2. *Police in Europe,* (based on Police in Europe Conference, Oporto, 1995) European Forum for Urban Security, Paris.

there is great scope for differences in implementation and a great many uncertainties. The latter may depend on the other players in local policy.

There is immense media and political pressure: the police are expected to produce results. No one could wish for anything else, but there has to be agreement as to the nature of these results. The number of arrests is an inadequate criterion of good policing. The way of operating, how witnesses and victims are handled and the amount of time spent in neighbourhoods taking an interest in the life of the community are also relevant indicators. Though undoubtedly more difficult to quantify than crude figures on the number of arrests, they are the guarantee of results in the long term.

The tendency is for the cultural model of police officers to be organised around serious crime and imitate the American supercop with all the latest gadgets and weapons: being someone committed to the fight against crime and especially serious crime, operating (posture, identity checks, arrests, and so forth) as if it were always a matter of the most serious type of case, treating run-of-the-mill incidents as if they were exceptional and every investigation as the investigation of the century. This is an attitude of war and struggle rather than one of crime management, prevention and reduction. The escalation in the arming of European police forces is disproportionate to the threats the police actually have to tackle. The special equipment some police units have is tending to become a norm common to all police forces. Budgets for equipment are soaring. We are far from a more accessible police force, an unarmed, preventive force based on information derived from social dialogue.

An increasing role

The role of the police is increasing in European countries. The police influential and in close partnership with the media for which, as we have seen, they are one of the main sources of inspiration. This partnership is dominated by the immediate present which plunges politicians into constant confusion. However, the time-scale of politics is not the same as that of the police or media. Reflection, dialogue and debate take time. What is to be done when there is an on-air demand for more reform, more spending and more enforcement? Politicians too often give in to emotion, forget debate and thus transform themselves into instruments of the media-police apparatus.

The police have become formidable agents for legislative change. Just as a few years ago lawyers had a monopoly on law and changes to it, so the police have now become leading agents of legislative change. Police demands concern not only changes in methods of investigation and the legal framework in which enquiries are conducted but also the nature and serving of sentences and the definition of charges. Police institutions have developed their own tools for conceptualising this new function. The European Union has recently taken the initiative of creating a European Police Academy. At the same time, more traditional, external, criminological research centres are receiving less political recognition. International institutions such as the United Nations, the Council of Europe and the European Union have taken on board and assisted this change. The number of meetings dominated by the police now outnumber those dominated by lawyers, judges and criminologists. One cannot regret this change since security issues should concern more and more players in the field, but this observation should also be a warning against the dangers of an unfortunate chain reaction. If we elevate the viewpoint of the police to the status of "absolute truth", then we risk ending up with a greatly impoverished understanding of society.

Are the police in the best position to discuss crime?

Police without borders

European and international co-operation is amplifying the risk of creating a police "complex" which will become autonomous.

Europol and the European Police Academy are the foundations of co-operation on serious crime issues among police forces in the European Union. There will be a tendency to become accustomed to the working habits of other forces within these authorities but, above all, a common doctrine and a common approach to problems will be developed.

There are also contacts between police forces on the ground. Border areas have for long given rise to joint police operations. International operations also contribute to such harmonisation. The war in Kosovo saw the setting-up of an international police force under the aegis of the United Nations to which thirty-three countries contributed.

The political unification of Europe will certainly accelerate this change. In the same way as we are setting up integrated armed forces, we are setting up police corps working on crossborder crime and mobile categories of the population. These prospects make it urgent to set up a corps of European prosecutors, because the question of how the police are to be controlled arises. Police forces will remain subject to the corpus of human rights, but to which institutions will citizens have access to have police abuses stopped?

European judicial systems

Judicial systems across Europe are among the unbeloved of the modernisation of security policies. The recruitment of judges and their assistants carries little weight in electoral campaigns. This inadequacy is undoubtedly a significant factor in the poor functioning of the criminal justice system as a whole. More police in theory means that more cases will be brought before the courts; the same is true if the opportunities for bringing proceedings and making complaints are increased. And yet the administrations of police and judiciary are doing nothing to bring them into line with each other.

However, spending on justice has increased in most western European countries. A French study[1] has compared Belgium, Germany, Spain, the United Kingdom,

---

1. "Budgets de la justice en Europe", *Mission de recherche Droit et justice,* ed. E. Douat, La Documentation française, Paris, 2001.

France and Italy for the years 1990-97 and found sharp increases, especially in Italy and Germany.

The justice budget
(according to French parameters)
(in billions of euros)

	1997	1990
France	6.35	4.2
Germany	13.52	6.74
United Kingdom	9.51	5.51
Italy	6.11	2.77
Spain	1.76	1.36
Belgium	1.15	0.72
Total	**38.4**	**21.3**
Average budget	**6.4**	**3.55**

© La Documentation française

These increases do not, however, offset the ground lost in some countries as is demonstrated by per capita spending in the respective countries.

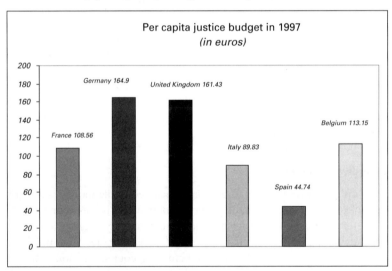

© La Documentation française

Common trends

European judicial systems are experiencing a number of concomitant changes. Firstly, there is talk of the increasing litigiousness of society, in the sense that the law we use to settle disputes is finding its natural, direct outlet in the criminal or civil courts (while mediation is still the principle of ordinary law in most countries and the resort to litigation the exception). Social relationships are being absorbed by the law. This is expressed in the mushrooming of disputes of every kind (civil, administrative, social law).

The indicator of the number of lawyers per capita reveals not only the trend towards litigiousness but also the ability of populations to settle disputes out of court. The latter theory is confirmed by the countries of southern Europe where there are large numbers of lawyers and court cases are contained.

Country	Population	Number of lawyers	Inhabitants per lawyer	Lawyers per 100 000
Germany	82 000 000	100 000	820	122
Austria	8 000 000	3 800	2 105	47.5
Belgium	10 000 000	4 104	2 437	41
Denmark	5 500 000	3 988	1 379	72.5
Spain	40 000 000	114 000	351	285
Finland	5 000 000	1 476	3 388	29.5
France	60 000 000	30 500	1 967	50.8
Greece	10 500 000	26 000	404	247.6
Netherlands	16 000 000	7 800	2 051	48.8
Ireland	3 800 000	8 000	475	210.5
Italy	58 000 000	115 000	504	198.3
Luxembourg	455 000	806	565	177.1
Portugal	10 000 000	16 828	594	168.3
Sweden	9 000 000	3 238	2 779	36
United Kingdom	52 500 000	95 650	549	182.2

© Documentation française

Generally speaking, taking matters to court, and in particular, civil disputes, are proliferating. We can also speak in terms of an over-criminalisation of social life. Criminal legislation is increasing at the same rate as other forms of control are disappearing. Types of behaviour that could be dealt with under the civil law are increasingly being brought within the scope of the criminal law.

Furthermore, the judicial structures dealing with both civil and criminal law are tending to favour collective disputes, without forward management and with less meaningful decisions that are increasingly based on automatic proceedings. The quality of judicial decisions is showing the effects of this. Citizens continue to feel alienated by legal terminology. Generally speaking, speeding up proceedings is the order of the day in both civil and criminal procedure. In recent years, all European countries have reformed procedures in order to reduce delays and bring cases to court more quickly. This means that, based on the principle that the courts are not handing down judgments quickly enough, proceedings are being pruned in various ways and investment is being made in the computerisation of procedures, particularly with respect to communication between police and judiciary. The "Justice for all" plan sets the objective of reducing the period within which a juvenile goes to trial from 142 to 63 days.[1] The selection criteria are being increased so that cases arrive in court, with alternative channels being put in place. Such channels use staff recruited according to less stringent criteria. Former solicitors, retired barristers and retired police officers are being called upon to settle minor disputes.

Decriminalisation is the other major proposal. This movement, which involves decriminalising offences so that they can be dealt with by other, more summary, channels, is on-going in European legal systems, which, on the other hand, continue to produce criminal legislation to deal with new types of behaviours or more closely regulate the activity of the courts.

It goes without saying that this may result in the rights of the defence being seriously undermined (less time to prepare the defence case, lack of social investigations, etc.). The most flagrant expression of this trend is guilty verdicts being immediately followed by sentencing or a decision not to impose a sentence, at best by a judge, but usually by prosecutors, or by courts sitting at night. It is unfortunate to note that such procedural short-cuts are applied to petty offences involving the poor and legally disadvantaged. Some consider this talking of a two-tier system of justice which fosters the feeling of injustice among these populations. Institutions may thus also generate violence by the way they operate.

The reign of public prosecutors

The second trend in European judicial systems is the appearance or consolidation of a figure mid-way between judiciary and police: the public prosecutor. The common law countries have gradually introduced public prosecutors; the Roman law countries have given them ever more powers. Placed in a position that enables them to gauge the level of activity of both the courts and the police, prosecutors have acquired powers to direct and select cases and which increase decision-making on the pretext of not burdening the courts with minor cases. Never mind their independent status, their functional flexibility makes them indispensable to the smooth running of the criminal justice system. In Germany, the *Staatsanwalt* can, with the agreement of the court, caution offenders, requiring them to pay damages, make a donation, do community service or help someone. Almost 47% of cases are now dealt with by public prosecutors. The French public prosecutor has the same type of powers independent of the bench. In the United Kingdom, the Crown Prosecution Service supervises the system of cautioning by the police, which accounts for 25% of solved crime.

---

1. "Justice for all plan", op.cit.

Public prosecutors are becoming the partners of other institutions involved in crime issues and are involved in defining crime prevention policy. They are becoming the partners of local crime reduction coalitions and local authorities. This development has been accelerated under the effect of both petty and more organised crime. Nascent European policies to combat organised crime are also contributing to the growing prominence of prosecutors on the national and international scene.[1]

Community justice

The term "community justice" refers both to the measures taken to speed up proceedings by simplifying them and to those taken to facilitate access to the courts for small claims. Justice is being decentralised and new types of places created in which there are people specialising in certain types of dispute, such as violence against women, vandalism and forms of antisocial behaviour that cause a deterioration in quality of life in cities. Judges are sometimes present, but prosecutors and mediators always are.

Similarly, some forms of justice close to inhabitants and their customs are increasingly recognised, although they represent a break with official models. Thus, within the French judicial system, justice in Polynesia and New Caledonia takes material constraints and also local customs into account. New Zealand and Canada have worked particularly hard on this issue in order to take into account earlier forms of justice specific to ethnic groups, such as the Yukon Family Court, which observes the native Indian form of discussion, namely the circle.

The specialisation of some forms of justice in particular types of dispute is another such international initiative. The introduction of "drug courts" or "family chambers" aims to make the professionals involved, notably judges, better qualified to deal with cases and therefore more effective. The reorganisation of juvenile justice in Europe is another example of this.

The United Kingdom has set up 154 multidisciplinary teams in local authorities ("youth offending teams") composed of representatives of the police, the probation service, social services, education, the health services and other local agencies. The function of the teams is to co-ordinate local action with respect to juveniles, provide the courts with information, manage community service sentences, supervise released prisoners and carry out all the tasks inherent in probation work. The teams allocate tasks to the person best able to deal with the immediate problem. In Portugal, the child and youth protection commissions in each municipality, composed of representatives of a number of institutions,[2] become involved when the prevention services are unable to act effectively.

---

1. Committee of Ministers Recommendation No. R (2000) 19 on the role of public prosecution in the criminal justice system, Council of Europe.
2. The commission is composed of representatives of many institutions: recreational bodies, youth associations, the police, citizens appointed by the municipality, social workers, psychologists, health workers, lawyers, the city geographically concerned, social security, education, the health services, charitable associations, recruitment agencies, parents' associations, sports and cultural associations.

Community justice seeks to provide redress and mediate between victim and offender. The Halt programme in the Netherlands brings in the victim of offences by juveniles aged between 12 and 18. The procedure takes place at police level. Young people are given the opportunity to apologise by doing work in compensation or another sort of work related to the nature of the offence. There is no legal record of the offence if the duty to perform is fulfilled. Mediation is seen as a way of avoiding minor offences reaching the courts. The idea is both to relieve the burden on the courts and avoid proceedings resulting in too much re-offending (the second argument is rarely spoken of openly, but very present in people's minds!). This type of work is very promising and should become an essential component of justice systems.

Justice and poverty

The access of the poor to the justice system and, more broadly, to law is a growing issue throughout the world. The assistance of a defence lawyer, setting-up procedures for settling land-use disputes and family problems are all crucial issues.

Poor countries do not have the means to set up and ensure access to justice systems comparable to those in the developed countries.[1] This issue affects not only the developing countries, but is also clear in the financial difficulties experienced by legal aid systems in richer countries.

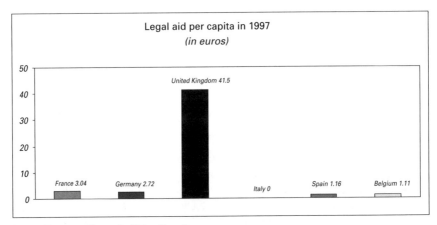

Source: European Forum for Urban Security

Levels of spending on legal aid in the rich countries are still very low. They should be increased to take into account Article 47 of the Charter of Fundamental Rights of the European Union, soon to be included in the European Convention on Human Rights.[2] However, such spending already accounts for 20% of the justice budget in France, for example, and is rising rapidly. It is closely connected with the development of victims' rights and, as these rights are increasingly being

---

1. *Justice and poverty*, UNDP Habitat, European Forum for Urban Security, Paris.
2. Article 47 of the charter: "… legal aid shall be made available to those who lack sufficient resources insofar as such aid is necessary to ensure effective access to justice".

affirmed, everything is in place for a sharp increase in legal aid. Is it not necessary to rethink procedures in the medium term, make the first level less formal and foster access? There is no doubt that community justice and mediation are possible solutions that respect the requirement for quality justice.

To this question is added the issue of the content of poverty alleviation policies. Is economic development sufficient to reach the poor gradually and bring them out of poverty? The answer is "no" for western Europe, where poverty has been rising for some years, and it is also "no" for eastern Europe, where the benefits of growth are insufficient to improve the situation in the medium term.

Social policies and combating exclusion should also cover developing access to the law through access to dispute and conflict settlement mechanisms appropriate to levels of development. This is not to seek to distinguish rich from poor and set up separate facilities for one and the other, but to take account of the fact that European justice systems are built on the principle of equality, but do not operate in an egalitarian fashion, and that there should be a proactive policy to correct this inequality. The need for justice is not satisfied by the criminal justice system in its present form.

IV. Violence and personal responsibility

Aspects of the individual

Our age has seen a decrease in the "community spirit" or the idea that the collective interest should prevail over the individual. The fierce battle for human rights has indirectly contributed to the rehabilitation of the individual, but, as so often happens, the pendulum has swung too far, in the sense that it has resulted in a degree of disinvestment in the general interest. "When it comes to a choice between my interests and the interests of society, I do my best to hang on to my advantages." A great many modernisation processes in European countries are blocked by this attitude. The organisations that represent the collective interest have also weakened and been transformed into service organisations in order to keep their members. The definition of the general interest is no longer clear. An illustration of this in the European Union is given by the debate on the notion of public service that would to some extent result in a *de facto* preservation of that service with respect to market forces. The compromise has been found in the guise of "services of general economic interest".[1]

The rise of individualism, the extreme attention paid to the individual and the constant search for personal involvement also go hand-in-hand with the appearance of the technical means that enable individuality to be expressed. Individual desire is no longer anonymous and is expressed ever more directly, in particular through the media, which are forcing politicians to invent a new discourse expressive of these innovations. Forms of democracy seek to be direct, with no intermediaries. The Internet is also a purveyor of this vision of the micro prevailing over the macro.

As this individualising trend gains force, the search for contact with the other is the constant refrain of political and social debate. Proximity, exchange, sharing and pragmatism are the values demanded to which institutional mechanisms attempt to give expression. This is resulting in a reassessment of the idea of delegating certain missions to the state. It is not that we oppose the state's mission to provide essential services to the community, but it is accountable to us as if the missions delegated could at any moment be revoked. The same demand is made of all the services provided by the state, including justice, the police and security. The performance of these missions in their present form is being challenged.

The challenge is all the stronger because recourse to the law is spreading rapidly throughout society. The rate of increase in legal aid, the huge growth in means

---

1. Article 36 of the Charter of Fundamental Rights of the European Union.

of access to the law and the great expansion in the number of lawyers are all pressures arguing in favour of a more efficient system in which individuals find their full place, useful for the maintenance of the social bond. We have to invent a form of justice that repairs and facilitates exchange, personal commitment and individual responsibility.

We knew this instinctively, we now know it scientifically. The more attention is paid to individuals, their history, their affective and psychological constituents, their social and economic involvement, the more sure we are of being able to help those individuals join the world of sustainable development, the world of personal involvement from which their behaviour has removed them.

"Rejoining the world" applies to both offender and victim. We have seen that current efforts are encountering two obstacles: first, the delays of the justice system which will never be reduced beyond a certain point, and second, inequality in the supply of victim support within cities and countries and between countries. This also applies to offenders

Constituents of the individual

The resurgence of individualism, the independence of the individual in relation to predetermined economic and social affiliations, is forcing us to pay more attention to the symptoms that may lead individuals to commit violence against others or against themselves. Criminology is telling us more about the factors that lead to acts of violence, and current policies focus increasingly on the goal of identifying "vulnerable" people, "populations at risk" and "children predisposed to violent behaviour".

The World Health Organisation has made a table of individual risk factors showing the complexity of the person's environment and the extraordinary possibilities we have of increasing the number of means of re-establishing a balanced relationship between the individual and her or his environment.

It is the same type of inventory as the United Nations drew up at the 10th UN Congress on the Prevention of Crime and Treatment of Offenders when it underlined the poverty and unemployment resulting from social exclusion, dysfunctional families, racial discrimination and the deterioration of urban environments and social bonds, to which might be added factors such as firearms, alcohol and drugs.

These observations have brought in their wake school-targeted policies that seek to identify more accurately the children affected by a number of these factors and inveterate young offenders for whom comprehensive programmes seek to respond to all the inadequacies in their upbringing. More broadly, such instruments for analysing the many causes of violence can help us identify the main themes of prevention policies in Europe. The instruments are not exhaustive, but are guides to the exchange of dialogue that restorative justice, discussed further on, should bring about.

Factors increasing young people's risk of perpetrating violence

Individual level
History of aggression
History of abuse
Social cognitive deficits
Impulsivity/hyperactivity
Hopelessness/depression
Learning difficulties
Drug and alcohol use
Family and close environment level
Exposure to family conflict
Harsh physical punishment or neglect
Involvement with delinquent peers
Poor academic achievements/early academic failure
Community level
Socio-economic marginalisation
Availability of firearms
Presence of gangs
Drug trafficking
Lack of social networks
Societal level
Cultural norms supportive of violence
Income inequality
State corruption and impunity

Source: *World report on violence and health*, WHO, 2002

Individual responsibility

The state must retain the monopoly of violence. This is one of the fundamental principles without which the sustainable development of a society is impossible. Force does not, however, guarantee security, the components of which are infinitely more complex. Prevention, combating exclusion, and reintegration are huge areas over which the state does not have a monopoly. As an essential partner, the state must therefore give itself the means of fostering the participation of all in reducing insecurity.

The wealth of European states has generated a highly developed system of services whose cost is born by the national community as a whole. Such systematised mutual insurance has been seriously attacked in recent years in the name of liberalism. The excesses of liberalism in recent years have been just as bad as the bureaucratic excesses of the welfare state model. The disappearance of some public services represents considerable social and economic costs. The privatisation of prisons was seen as a way of improving the service and saving large amounts of money, but has resulted in the collapse of services, and practices that violate prisoners' rights.

What is left today of this offensive and the debates that went with it is undeniably the question of individual responsibility. Giving individuals back the quality of possessors of rights and duties is without any doubt the thread running through many actions undertaken in different domains.

This quality not only begs the question, but is also a management principle of a number of public policies whose effectiveness largely depends on the personal involvement of every individual.

Every possible measure may be taken to try to eliminate fare-dodging on public transport – cameras, electronic sensors, staff – but nothing is as effective as the collective awareness of users and disapproval of fare-dodgers. Neighbourhood police patrols can be increased in an attempt to prevent burglary, but it is more likely to be reduced if local people agree to concern themselves with the house next door when its occupants are out.

With respect to young people, consensus has been reached in Europe as to the responsibility of parents and their essential role in education. This theme goes back to the 19th century and seems to well up when doubts grow as to the ability of the state to perform its role of maintaining order. We are learning that parenting is not innate, that it has to be socialised and can be brought into a process of training and awareness. We cannot forget, however, that the family is competing with others involved in education, that is, peers and the media.

The United Kingdom Crime and Disorder Act of 1999 is a perfect example of this highlighting of parental authority. Parents may be ordered to intervene with respect to the behaviour of their children aged between 10 and 17 in order to prevent bad conduct and the repetition of delinquent acts. Such orders may include various duties, such as taking the children to school, taking advice or following a one-week to three-month course. Failure to perform results in the imposition of a fine.

The French philosopher Yves Michaud[1] has described an historical period in which "the individual is dismissed in favour of laws, structures and the community … subjects with no perceptible substance … grappling with force fields and regulations". He believes it is necessary to reinstate individuals, with their feelings and passions and therefore with the concomitant responsibility. The individual as a product of history or the individual controlling her or his history is a constantly debated dilemma.

What is new at this time of economic and political upheaval is that the individual is being rediscovered not only as a consumer, payer or producer but also as a sentient being of flesh and blood. A few months ago, a German minister was insulted by a passer-by about his private life and hit the person; more recently, during an election campaign, a French politician slapped a child who was rummaging in his pocket. These two scenes deserve to be noted, not in order to make them a principle of government for Europe, but as the eruption of physical confrontation, perhaps an encounter, in a world that is used to permanent compromise and evasion. The public overwhelmingly approved the reactions of the two politicians. These are anecdotes that say a great deal about the sudden rediscovery of personal responsibility.

---

1. *Changements dans la violence*, Editions Odile Jacob, France, 2002.

This should be remembered more often when we are talking about globalisation, the market and the need for development. We should remember it with respect to crime issues. It is surprising to learn that a number of countries have passed legislation to enable witnesses to remain anonymous in order to encourage them to testify in court. Life in some neighbourhoods is regarded as making it difficult for victims to give evidence because of their environment and the risk of reprisals. France has just passed such a provision. England has for some years had the "Crimestoppers trust" programme – initially designed for the poorest neighbourhoods with high levels of insecurity – based on anonymous telephone calls to Scotland Yard, which are rewarded if the information makes it possible to put an end to unlawful activities. One may wonder about the contradiction between the wish to affirm individual responsibility and measures that make witnesses disappear as legal subjects (name, address, etc.).

Personal responsibility should be accompanied by direct individual involvement in areas "delegated to the state". We need to examine the possibility of making delegated powers revocable if citizens manifest the wish to become personally involved.

Offenders and punishment

Individualising sentencing, taking into account the characteristics of individuals so as to help them find their place in the community and distance them from the psychological, social and economic conditions that made them separate themselves from the community for a time by committing an offence, this is the organising principle of the system of punishment, a principle based on balancing society's legitimate demand for punishment and the offender's future.

This is the ideal. The reality is very different: punishments have increased in number, there is little diversity in them, and they have incontestably lost their meaning. The considerable increase in criminal legislation, poor administration of the machinery that hands down sentences, and the crisis of legitimacy in the way power is exercised or the life rules for society are upheld are all factors in the inflation and loss of meaning of punishment.

The rule of law and its enforcement have become increasingly artificial exercises in which the correlation between offence and punishment has disappeared. How can a meaningful scale of punishments be maintained, including for behaviour with more and more immeasurable social consequences? The corruption of politicians is making it even more difficult to explain to young people that theft in a supermarket should be proscribed; the impunity financiers and politicians give themselves is reducing the impact of a young thief's appearance in court.

The poor results our systems have obtained, measurable in re-offending and repetition[1] can be explained by two observations: prison is still the basis of the

---

1. According to the United States Bureau of Justice statistics on recidivism for 2002, two-thirds of those leaving American prisons re-offend within three years; in United Kingdom, a Home Office study found that half of those who left prison in 1997 re-offended within two years.

59

punishment system and this ubiquitous presence is hindering the conception of other, more flexible, forms of punishment better adapted to the victim's interests and the rehabilitation of the offender.

Prison

The *UN Global report on crime and justice* notes that the use of prison is tending to increase steadily but, what is more important, it is in no way correlated with the nature and organisation of legal systems, is unrelated to crime rates in the country concerned and bears no correlation with the level of development.

One may wonder what use is served by the efforts our criminal justice systems have made, particularly in the training of judges. A study conducted by the Council of Europe in 1996 covering thirty-six countries, which will be updated in 2003, found that the main cause of overcrowding in prisons was longer sentences.

What is the present ranking of countries with respect to imprisonment? According to the Council of Europe figures collected every year and used by the United Kingdom Home Office, to which they have added figures from other countries,[1] the average number of prisoners per 100 000 inhabitants in the European Union is 87. England, Portugal, Scotland and Spain top the list. It should be remembered that Portugal and Spain have the lowest crime rates. While the average is 87 in the European Union, it is 180 in eastern Europe, excluding the Russian Federation, where the figure is 729 (in the United States it is 685).

Who goes to prison?

The largest proportion of people sent to prison are in the 16-27 age group; most of them are illiterate and have no professional qualifications. Some incomplete studies in Germany and Italy corroborate French observations arrived at on the basis of 2 300 persons going to prison found that 55% suffer from one or more types of psychiatric problems, in particular over-developed aggression and anger.[2] The United Kingdom has found that more than 70% of male prisoners present more than two serious symptoms.[3] This situation is partly a result of major changes in psychiatric services which now work more in the community so that prison is gradually replacing psychiatric hospitals. To such deplorable individual situations is added the handicap of overcrowding, one immediate effect of which is to increase tension in prisons.

Prison is above all a solution of last resort. It is essential in serious cases and, in particular, cases of violence and those posing a serious threat to society. It is, however, little used in such cases as 77% of those entering prison in United Kingdom are there for non-violent offences!

---

1. Roy Walmsley, *World prison population list – Findings 166* (third edition), UK Home Office, online publication (see: http://www.homeoffice.gov.uk/rds/pdfs/r166.pdf).
2. France, General Directorate of Health, July 2002.
3. "Reducing re-offending by ex-prisoners", Social Exclusion Unit report, London, July 2002.

Prisons as schools of violence

The observatory set up by the International Centre for Prison Studies in London[1] gives the overcrowding rates of all the prisons in Europe. The majority of prison systems *are* overcrowded, the average being 1.5 prisoners per place. This overcrowding rate, in addition to what it suggests about prisoners' comfort, expresses the permanent failure of the principle that rehabilitation should govern sentencing. The facilities are never sufficient to assist rehabilitation, and this in part explains high failure rates when people leave prison.

According to Sylvia Casale, president of the Council of Europe's European Committee for the Prevention of Torture and Inhuman or Degrading Treatment or Punishment, the biggest problem is overcrowding in prisons, and it is universal. This means conditions are deteriorating even where they were good at the outset, and this applies to space, hygiene and food. This generates pressure and violence and therefore greater insecurity. Prisons are still schools of violence, and violence is generated by the institution.

Prisons are expensive

The argument that prisons are expensive has little weight in limiting the imposition of custodial sentences. The liberalism at work in some countries has not faced all the aspects of the question. According to a United Nations report, a prisoner costs US$150 000, which is about the same as one equipped police officer, and longer sentences can only increase this cost. In England, the Howard League for Penal Reform estimates that a prisoner costs £500 a week and that the cost of a new prison is the same as the cost of a district hospital. In 2002, California devoted 18% of its budget to prisons and less than 1% to higher education. The privatisation of prisons has been seen as a solution to this financial burden. It is little applied in Europe; the problems of the profitability of the structure linked to the regular arrival of more prisoners is not part of the culture of the criminal justice system. The building of new prisons is on the agenda of most governments.

Alternative measures, but to what?

The poor results our systems have obtained, measurable by re-offending and repetition rates, can largely be explained by one observation: prison is the central pivot of criminal justice and the basis of the system of punishment. The existence of prisons and the ease with which people can be sent there compromise efforts not only to make more effective a few other, more flexible, punishments better adapted to victims' interests and the reform of offenders but also compromises the development of other alternatives.

In France in 2001, of 580 000 judgments, only 60 000 involved alternative sentences and these included only 10 000 community service orders. The existence of prison as a last resort does not give the necessary stimulation to those managing

---

1. "World prison brief", International Centre for Prison Studies, Kings College London, online publication (see: http://www.prisonstudies.org).

alternative punishments. The adult/young offender relationship cannot be established on the possibility of eliminating the other from the dialogue; at worst, there can be replacement or substitution, but not elimination. The existence of prison is a reminder of the ever-present possibility of elimination, and this limits the impact of alternative forms of punishment in the eyes of those involved.

A proactive policy should make it possible to limit the use of prison. Andrew Coyle, the Director of the International Centre for Prison Studies, gives a few examples of such proactivism:

> In Denmark, on the other hand, the number of prisoners has been almost constant for the past twenty-five years. This is because that country has actually implemented the internationally recognised principle of using custodial sentences only when strictly necessary. To achieve this, sentencing policies have been regularly reviewed, for instance, in respect of drunken driving and minor property offences, and alternatives to prison expanded. Over a similar period of time Finland has set out in a determined way to reduce its prison population and has achieved this with no noticeable increase in crime rates. In many countries in eastern Europe a variety of alternatives to prison are already provided in legislation. These alternatives are appropriate for the needs of the region. What is required is encouragement to the judiciary to use these provisions and support for the administrative infrastructure to make sure that they are properly implemented. The Ministry of Justice in the Russian Federation currently has a number of important initiatives to help these things to happen. Similarly, in Latvia, recent developments in community service are to be applauded. *International Centre for Prison Studies (http://www.prisonstudies.org)*

Alternative forms of punishment are mainly based on the promise (giving one's word) not to re-offend, with measures to support that promise. The duties imposed on the offender take into account the offender's psychological, social and financial situation and are above all adapted in accordance with the offender's personal development.

The other major family of alternative measures focuses on the idea of mediation between offender and victim, a process which concentrates more on the futures of victim and offender. Mediation may be decided upon within or outside the judicial sphere, by the police.

It has to be recognised, however, that the use of alternatives to prison does not reduce prison sentences. Alternatives are usually imposed on persons who at one time would not have been punished at all. This observation is very revealing of the rise in power of the security apparatus in most countries.

The attempt to personalise sentences is therefore only in its infancy. This principle, proclaimed just after the war by European criminologists (some of whom had themselves been political prisoners), has diversified some criminal measures, notably with respect to the ways in which some illnesses and types of addiction are dealt with, but people's social, family and economic situations are still largely ignored.

The final declaration of the 10th UN Congress on the Prevention of Crime and Treatment of Offenders may remain a pious hope for many years to come "We commit ourselves to according priority to containing the growth and overcrowding of pre-trial and detention prison populations, as appropriate, by promoting safe and effective alternatives to incarceration".[1]

The earlier declaration of the Cairo Congress (9th UN congress on the same subject) was more affirmative, committing states to reducing the number of prisoners. We are now content to reduce overcrowding.

Victims

The power citizens delegate to the state to ensure their security and the safeguarding of their lives and property has been translated into police and judicial procedures which have organised an exclusive confrontation between offenders and the state. The decision to take action, the decision to take cases to court and the nature of sentences have become the exclusive preserve of the judicial machinery. It has gradually been realised that victims have been excluded from their "cases". This process of abdication and renunciation was to a great extent caused by the insurance system which, by putting a price on the harm suffered, encouraged victims to be passive. While such delegation may be satisfactory for a certain number of offences, it can be very frustrating and psychologically devastating for the victim.

The settlement of cases involving violence has shown that victims do not want only to receive compensation, they also want to be involved in proceedings and meet the person responsible for their injury. The cause of violence against women has contributed a great deal to this awareness and to a number of legislative changes.

Furthermore, the compensation the victim receives when judgment is handed down comes long after the event, whereas something should be done as soon as possible to help the victim overcome the distress caused. Providing material assistance, restoring the home to its former condition and offering legal advice and psychological counselling are now included in public policy as well as in the work of the voluntary sector.

Victims international

Policies to provide victims with immediate assistance are now widespread and involve all aspects of personal protection. Teams that are an integral part of emergency-service teams may intervene at any time to deal with the results of disasters; this innovation has a fortunate consequence for the development of international co-operation by enabling the intervention of multinational teams in the event of disasters involving victims of different nationalities. Such group interventions should be developed, and necessitate work on legal terminology. Internationalisation is all the more necessary since, as the European Commission noted in July 1999, more than 200 million Europeans, that is, one in two, travel within the community and every year 200 000 students travel for the purposes of their studies.[2]

1. Vienna Declaration on Crime and Justice: Meeting the Challenges of the 21st Century, United Nations Congress, April 2000.
2. Communication to the European Parliament, the Council of Europe and the EU Economic and Social Committee, 14 July 1999.

As early as 1985, the Congress of Local and Regional Authorities of Europe put victims at the heart of insecurity reduction policies.[1] In addition to its basic humanity, this approach is also a means of reducing the feeling of insecurity disseminated by victims who are left without support or assistance. As early as 1987, the Committee of Ministers of the Council of Europe adopted the principle of nineteen measures aimed at developing victim support policies.[2]

The question of victims is at the centre of concerns in the area of freedom, security and justice put in place at the Tampere Summit of the member states of the European Union.[3]

Since then, the Commission has adopted a fourfold approach: prevention of victimisation, victim support, the victim's place in criminal proceedings and the compensation of victims. The compensation of victims is the subject of priority work by the Commission, which has launched European consultations on the basis of a Green Paper.[4]

Victim surveys

The prevention of victimisation represents a certain change in the question that had its origin in British studies that showed that certain persons, such as elderly women, and also certain places, were more likely to be victims than others (UK Home Office study on burglary). The common denominator of these potential victims appears to be their temporary or permanent weakness. Preventing people from becoming victims therefore involves identifying places or people (such as tourists in airport crowds, foreign tourists in towns, etc.), and concentrating attention and protection on them. Some people also see in this approach a way of managing police forces.

With respect to preventive measures, much attention has been focused on developing knowledge about and access to the law. Italy has developed school syllabuses on law in order to strengthen the fight against the Mafia. France has distributed teaching modules to schools in the form of exhibitions in order to develop knowledge about justice. It is not surprising that one of the main obstacles noted by the promoters of such initiatives is legal terminology itself.

The inequality of victims

Nevertheless, despite many international declarations, victim support has yet to become a component of public action. While it can be said that justice provides relative equality of access, if only by virtue of equal cover of a country's territory,

---

1. CLRAE Resolution 163 on security in European towns, adopted on 16 October 1985, Council of Europe.
2. Committee of Ministers Recommendation No. R (87) 21 on assistance to victims and the prevention of victimisation, Council of Europe.
3. Towards a Union of Freedom, Security and Justice (conference, Tempere, 15-16 October 1999), European Counci36
4. European Commission Green Paper on compensation to crime victims (COM (2001) 536), 28 September 2001.

victim support is still very scattered and diluted in social and legal policy provisions. This is partly because the movement mainly involves non-governmental organisations and volunteers receiving sometimes uncertain funding from the authorities. Few countries have set up agencies at local level to co-ordinate all the machinery in this field. This was the observation made by two researchers who had examined the deployment of the Committee of Ministers Recommendation No. R (1985) 11 on the position of the victim in the framework of criminal law and procedure.[1]

In fact, the European Union still has widely varying systems for dealing with victims. In different countries the list of offences that open the right to compensation of the victim varies, as does the amount of compensation, and in some countries persons who are not resident in the European Union are excluded. The European Court of Justice gave the initial impetus for the necessary harmonisation of European legislation in the form of a judgment requiring the French Government to take responsibility for a British tourist who had been the victim of an attack on French territory.[2] Fifteen years on, much still remains to be achieved.

Victim versus citizen?

Victim support policies were first introduced with respect to crime, terrorism in particular. The introduction of reception arrangements has resulted in the emergence of victims "of every kind": people complaining of the malfunctioning of a government department or public service and people who are victims of their own negligence. The notion of the victim has become universal and its extension goes hand in hand with the great increase in the number of court cases, the "judicialisation" of social relationships. At one time or another in our daily lives we will all fall into the category of victims.

There is a danger that being a victim will become a new political category replacing that of citizen. This would radically change the relationship we have with politics. This is perhaps one explanation of the sudden appearance in Europe of populist groups born of the "grievances" of individuals who are eternal victims to whom they claim to provide an immediate remedy. Their solution usually consists of making new victims but of a different nationality! This perpetual status of victim may explain the deterioration in levels of satisfaction with the efforts being made. Despite the setting-up of victim support (1.5 million people dealt with every year), victim satisfaction in United Kingdom fell from 67% in 1994 to 58% in 2000.[3]

The quantitative approach is the one favoured by politicians for improving the criminal justice system and responding to a social demand for security whose terrible complexity we have seen. Incoherence is the conclusion we must draw.

---

1. E. H. Hoegen, M. E. I. Brienen, *Victims of crime in 22 European criminal justice systems: the implementation of Recommendation (85) 11 of the Council of Europe on the position of the victim in the framework of criminal law and procedure, dissertation,* University of Tilburg Nijmegen, Wolf Legal Productions, Netherlands, 2000.
2. Case 186/87, *Ian William Cowan v. Trésor public,* [1989] European Court Reports 195.
3. Sir Robin Auld, *Review of the criminal courts in England and Wales,* online publication (see: http://www.criminal-courts-review.org.uk) October 2001.

And we might suspect that therein lies the source of the loss of credibility of criminal justice systems. More serious still, the incoherence may be transformed into citizens' disaffection with the democratic system. Belgium experienced one of the most serious institutional crises in its history as a result of a criminal case. And it is not the Final Declaration of the Vienna Congress of the United Nations that is going to give the impetus to serious mobilisation: "We emphasise the responsibility of each state to establish and maintain a fair, responsible, ethical and efficient criminal justice system.[1]

An active citizenship

The disaffection of citizens is often put forward as a major cause of the crisis in political representation in our democracies. Disaffection with politics is not reflected in participation in NGOs or local voluntary bodies, nor when citizens take part in the workings of justice. Every year, 200 000 people serve on juries in criminal cases in the United Kingdom. In France, some 20 000 volunteers take part in the work of juvenile and assize courts. The association of professional judges with citizen-judges has been little explored by promoters of reform in justice systems. An inventory should be made of all the examples of the involvement of citizens provided by justice systems in the various countries of Europe.

Becoming involved, not waiting for someone else to provide the service needed, not expecting the government to do everything, directly tackling problems that disturb one's own and other people's daily lives, confronting offenders and engaging in dialogue, helping to resolve and address problems – numerous actions undertaken by NGOs and public institutions are built on these foundations.

The Council of Europe has indicated avenues for personal involvement several times, advocating that the public be strongly encouraged "to play a practical part in the non-custodial treatment of offenders" and the voluntary sector and associations to develop non-custodial measures.[2] The European Urban Charter, a reference in many later resolutions and recommendations, speaks of "close co-operation between the police and the local community".[3]

Personal involvement is encountering two obstacles, the monopoly of force exercised by the police and individual freedoms. How can one become involved as a volunteer in security operations that may result in arrest? To what extent should one become involved in activity that may give access to confidential information about another person? Collaboration with an official agency working in the field of security or crime always involves a risk that the limits will be overstepped. Below are a few examples of such voluntary involvement and attempts to supervise them.

---

1. Vienna Declaration on Crime and Justice, op. cit.
2. Committee of Ministers Recommendation No. R (1983) 7 on participation of the public in crime wpolicy, Council of Europe.
3. CLRAE Resolution adopting the European Urban Charter, 18 March 1992, Council of Europe.

In May 2002, the Attorney General of the United States announced the creation of a corps of volunteers to work with the police and which would carry out tasks so that police officers would always be available to be on the "front line". They undertake no tasks requiring them to take an oath, but answer the telephone and fill in files. "The work may not be exciting, but it is essential." The initiative is being taken in the framework of a broader initiative, the USA Freedom Corps, which is designed to encourage a series of citizens' initiatives developing new possibilities for citizens to become involved in serving their community. The bases of this type of initiative are not new in the United States, citizen involvement being a founding feature of the United States Republic. Such involvement has always tended to limit government services. One may wonder, however, whether the approach respects private life. Access to police files provides a mine of information on the community, especially if the community is small.

Another example of personal involvement in prevention work: for several years now, groups of parents in several cities in northern Europe, notably Stockholm, have been taking turns at night visiting, particularly on Saturday nights, music venues frequented by their children. The common fear that motivates them is drug-taking and alcohol abuse, especially the road accidents they may lead to. Their visits are both to the young people themselves and the people managing the venues. Such an initiative inspired by parental responsibility raises a number of questions. The first is the degree of independence young people should have from their parents, and the second is that young people who really want to use forbidden substances or abuse alcohol will take refuge elsewhere. Furthermore, the parents' involvement in situations of conflict arising from trafficking requires a degree of control and preparation in order to avoid tension degenerating into violence. Finally, there is the question of private life and the information acquired about elements of the lives of young people where parents are not welcome.

The tackling of difficult situations is illustrated in another way in Rome by neighbourhood meetings of people infuriated by nuisance linked with drug-trafficking in their street. They decided to make use of drama and music activities to disturb the drug market and force dealers to move elsewhere. They were successful: the dealers left but, fortunately, the cultural activities continued.

The Swedish and Italian examples were strongly motivated by direct, powerful, personal interest. Their aim was not to assist the long-term resolution of a problem as the initiatives are not long-lasting. Most parents whose children no longer frequent nearby music clubs abandon their involvement. Similarly, the nature of the Rome initiative changed once the dealers had left the neighbourhood. Conversely, two other initiatives illustrate the durability of initiatives, each for different reasons.

The British "neighbourhood watch" schemes involve neighbours watching each other's homes when the occupants are away. In order to support the development of such initiatives, the police have decided to take them in hand, both to ensure that the right to private life is respected and to teach people to be more effective in their surveillance. Furthermore, an official is appointed in each neighbourhood and a national organisation federates the tens of thousands of neighbourhood

67

watches. A large number of training schemes has been developed to see that people's private lives are respected. Apart from the (varying) effectiveness of the action, the important point is that it brings together the will of many people to become involved for the benefit of the community and of immediate personal interests.

In 1997, the CLRAE gave its support to the participation of citizens in crime prevention through neighbourhood watch schemes or other initiatives encouraging citizens to defend their convictions and protect themselves and their property in collaboration with the authorities,[1] but a few months later it was speaking only in terms of citizens' initiatives to stand up for their beliefs,[2] a sign of the on-going debate on the depth of personal involvement in security issues.

In 2000 the European Crime Prevention Prize was awarded to the initiative of Moroccan fathers in a neighbourhood of the Dutch city of Rotterdam, who had decided to take charge of young people who were hanging about on the streets of the neighbourhood and causing incidents. The initiative had a dual motivation, aiming to put an end to the growing disapproval of the Moroccan community, which the rest of the community held responsible for delinquency, and also to meet the criticism that fathers were not involved in the upbringing of their children. They got together and set up a series of street-based activities in order both to exercise some control over the youngsters and help them with their schoolwork and cultural activities. The results were spectacular. The durability of the action is a result both of the residential stability of the community and the integration of the action in the local security plan adopted by the city. Such integration makes it possible to fund the actions.

This is another example of action motivated neither by direct personal interest nor by a desire to protect the community. One feels in it more a personal commitment to humanist values, personal references.

The aim of the mentoring schemes developed in the United Kingdom, for which one of the experiments has just been the subject of UK Home Office evaluation,[3] is for a trained mentor to work with a child experiencing problems integrating in the school community. It concerns primary school children identified by teachers. The mentors are volunteers recruited for a period of a year after a lengthy selection process. Their role is to take children out once a week, for a walk or to leisure and cultural activities. They try to jolt the child into feeling better about her/himself and more comfortable with other people. A certificate is awarded at the end of the course. Mentor recruitment campaigns are regularly launched in the media.

Every country has the legal and financial capabilities for implementing and supporting such actions, but every action is a reflection of cultural specificities.

---

1. CLRAE International Conference on Crime and Urban Insecurity in Europe: the Role and Responsibilities of Local and Regional Authorities, Erfurt, 26-28 February 1997, Council of Europe.
2. CLRAE Resolution 57 on crime and urban security in Europe, adopted on 5 June 1997, Council of Europe.
3. Ian St James Roberts and Clifford Samlal Singh "Mentors for primary school children with behaviour problems: an evaluation of the Change project", Finding 157, British Home Office.

Collaboration between citizens and the police is not well-regarded in most countries of southern and eastern Europe. Similarly, in the same countries, attempts at "self-managed watch" recall painful episodes in their history when policies of informing and denunciation were erected into a system of government.

It is this past which marks the difference with the general issue of involvement in democratic life and the development of one's community. The CLRAE has welcomed the development of self-help initiatives in the framework of the renaissance of local communities and the development of harmonious cities and has pointed out that such initiatives affected spheres likely to improve daily life in cities, such as health, the environment, employment, culture, ethnic and racial integration, and improving problem neighbourhoods. They stimulated solidarity, the economy and civic pride at local level. They were in part the result of a protest against an outside threat, of the lack of a key service for a group or neighbourhood and of a reaction to an urban renewal policy which had broken up traditional communities and social bonds. They provided new services, enhanced personal aptitudes and self-confidence, and helped to improve the functioning of local institutions.[1]

Restorative justice or the justice of dialogue

Restorative justice does not necessarily respect the imperatives of yield, but favours qualitative objectives that should give equal satisfaction to three parties in a process that may have several phases. The policy has three constituents: a community-based approach to justice, a policy that focuses on the individual, whether victim or offender, and the involvement of the community.

A three-way process

In theory, three parties are concerned in the investigation of a criminal case and its judgment: the offender, the victim and society. This trio has gradually emerged over time, but not in a very balanced fashion. The victim was very soon pushed to one side. The state soon became disembodied as cases and society became more complex. Little by little we have moved away from the trio formed on the basis of the transgression of a social norm.

Victims should be the prime focus of attention – and much has to be done to bring this about – but we also need to reintroduce the community, the immediate environment, the web of relationships and the urban entity in which the victim lives, which are also affected by the offence because they care about the victim or are concerned, and because their convictions are undermined or their common values flouted. The process initiated with the offender is therefore an exercise in explaining causes and reasons, a means of compensating for the harm suffered by the victim and giving grounds for not re-offending. Everyone should take part in this work in the course of which the representative of the community voices the

---

1. CLRAE Resolution 208 on self-help and community development in towns, 8 March 1989, Council of Europe.

community's emotion but also personifies its ability to help produce a positive out-comes in this process.

The resolution of the United Nations Vienna Congress passes somewhat rapidly over restorative justice but sums up effectively its considerable interest: it is a form of justice that would respect the rights, needs and interests of victims, offenders, communities and all other parties.[1] A resolution of the Economic and Social Council of the United Nations noted simply that the traditional response of the criminal justice system does not always provide an appropriate response within a reasonable time.[2] In a report published in October 2001, Sir Robin Auld goes further:[3]

> Restorative justice is fundamentally concerned with restoring social relationships, with establishing or re-establishing social equality in relationships. That is, relationships in which each person's rights to equal dignity, concern and respect are satisfied. What practices are required to restore the relationship at issue will, then, be context-dependent and judged against this standard of restoration. As it is concerned with social equality, restorative justice inherently demands that one attend to the nature of relationships between individuals, groups and communities. Thus, in order to achieve restoration of relationships, restorative justice must be concerned both with the discrete wrong and its relevant context and causes.

Supplementary or alternative?

This "other" dimension which characterises restorative justice is changing ways of thinking about the introduction of this new form of justice. It is no longer a question of finding ways of speeding-up the normal course of justice, as the European ministers of justice meeting in London recognised when they looked at ways of avoiding delays and noted that "extra-judicial methods of dispute resolution can reduce the volume of cases before the courts and provide citizens with more appropriate means of settling disputes".[4] The same debate has taken place in the United Nations Commission on Crime Prevention and Criminal Justice. The UN Secretary General noted that some countries, including the United States and the United Kingdom consider restorative justice to be complementary to the traditional system of justice rather than an alternative to it.[5] Other countries, realising the changed perspective of restorative justice, have put forward a compromise: "restorative justice would serve as a supplement to established criminal justice practices especially in areas where such practices had not functioned adequately".

We should add that the use of the word justice is misleading. We are not talking only about judicial institutions, but also the police and institutions responsible for enforcing sentences. The basic principle of this new policy is to restore meaning

---

1. Vienna Declaration on Crime and Justice, op. cit.
2. ECOSOC Resolution 1996/26 UN.
3. *Review of the Criminal Courts of England and Wales*, op. cit.
4. London Conference of European Ministers of Justice (8-9 June 2000) Council of Europe.
5. "Reform of the criminal justice system: achieving effectiveness and equity", report by the Secretary General of the United Nations, 7 January 2002.

to all the actors in criminal proceedings. These principles should be applied throughout social intervention on violence and crime.

A "proximity" process

The term *"proximité"* is used in France to refer to the establishment of justice centres in neighbourhoods particularly exposed to social, economic and integration problems. English-speaking countries prefer the term "community justice". The French reluctance to speak in terms of community justice has its source in the refusal of the French Republic to recognise the political existence of communities based on ethnicity or race. A rapprochement can nonetheless be made by pointing out that the term "community" above all reflects proximity to a district or neighbourhood.

The promoters of the movement in the United States tell us that community or neighbourhood justice brings all the actors in the criminal justice system and citizens together in order better to resolve neighbourhood problems. Interventions vary widely and should be adapted to actual problems on the ground. The movement, which began in the 1990s, started from the idea that a mass of disorders, antisocial behaviour and vandalism was preventing citizens from taking action on the most important questions. It was therefore urgent to deploy the actors of the criminal justice system on the ground and quickly improve citizens' quality of life. One action in Vermont brought together offenders and the citizens of a neighbourhood so that agreement could be reached on repairing the damage caused to the neighbourhood. In Oregon, the programme appoints prosecutors to particular neighbourhoods to settle problems of everyday life. In Massachusetts, the police have proposed a non-violence pact to the members of various gangs.

These experiments show that people in the criminal justice system want to play a role different from the one assigned them by their function or position. They are reversing perceptions of the seriousness of offences, while at the same time respecting the law and professional ethics. Antisocial behaviour is considered as important as aggravated theft.

This also reflects a conception of the work of public institutions that focuses more on the citizen. They take the view that citizens are also clients to whom the criminal justice system is accountable. They therefore want to see public confidence in judicial institutions increase.

This approach means that the various agencies have to agree to work together and, in particular, that social workers must agree to collaborate with prosecutors. The joint approach by different bodies is far more than a convenient partnership; it is a change in philosophy that is transforming centralised authorities into authorities that agree to take decisions on the basis of the actual situation on the ground and to extend their traditional mission (to arrest and bring to trial) by taking action on the way crime can affect victims and the community.

Since the 1990s, France has been involved in the same process, linking it with renovation projects for neighbourhoods with serious social problems. In this context, the French Ministry of Justice agreed to work in a number of cities and establish first of all local offices of the courts and subsequently justice centres called *Maisons de justice et du droit* (MJD) (Law and justice centres). The centres, which are designed to be close to the problems of individuals, include court services units, such as the probation service, juvenile protection services and representatives of the court registry involved in family issues. There are also assistance services for women and victims and mediation and conciliation services specific to juveniles and adults. The centres are jointly funded by the Ministry of Justice and local authorities. The services they offer depend on the ability of local actors to mobilise on this or that problem, but also on the ability of the courts, above all prosecutors, to become involved, although staffing problems limit their presence. The bench, such as judges of the juvenile court for whom such service is not compulsory, takes part according to their willingness, availability and belief in its usefulness. Lawyers have been involved in setting-up the centres. Differences in investment and available staff in different districts mean that the services offered vary widely, ranging from legal advice to mediation to court services.

The Netherlands also has a neighbourhood justice programme that includes the opening of centres in working class neighbourhoods with social problems.[1] There were nine centres by the end of 1999 based on teams composed of the prosecutor, the police, child protection services and rehabilitation and victim support services. Much of the centres' work is done with schools. While contacts with schools were previously the responsibility of the police, the neighbourhood justice centres have enabled the justice system to take over this relationship. This is also one of the aims of the promoters of community justice programmes in the United States.

In addition to established, co-ordinated programmes, there are many other initiatives in various countries. Prosecutors, often on an individual basis, have taken the initiative of going to meet citizens through the voluntary bodies and NGOs in their district, and in neighbourhoods. Such initiatives often result in co-operative action with precise objectives, notably in the area of family violence, violence against homosexuals and truancy.

Such involvement by the justice system is based on legal measures alternative to imprisonment, such as cautioning, notice, orders and injunctions, conditional suspended sentences, community service and compensation of victims.[2] Every legal system has these sorts of measures, and in many cases has had them for many years. Thus, in Germany, *Täter-Opfer Ausgleich* measures (bringing together offenders and victims) may be used at any stage in proceedings, including imprisonment. Nearly 60% of such measures concern violent acts.

We have seen, however, that the traditional system of justice does not have the means to take full advantage of them and make them effective and efficient. Only

---

1. J. C. Boutellier, "Right to the community, neighbourhood justice in the Netherlands", *European Journal on Criminal Policy and Research,* 1997.
2. See Committee of Ministers Recommendation No. R (2000) 22 on improving the implementation of the European rules on community sanctions and measures, Council of Europe.

involvement in the neighbourhood or community can give them real meaning. As Martin Wright has pointed out, there is no clear division between measures that come under the umbrella of restorative justice and those that do not; there is a spectrum that goes from the authoritarian to the democratic, by way of the uni-lateral.[1] Quality of life, authority, democracy, citizens, ground, neighbourhood, community, justice, these are the words that have to be brought together in order to reduce insecurity and violence. Another word should join them, namely, medi-ation. This is the second mechanism that restorative justice should implement.

A mediating process

There is no longer any question that mediation and its usefulness must be recog-nised. Here again, however, the objectives of mediation are interpreted differently. The Committee of Ministers of the Council of Europe sees mediation as a means of reducing the overloading of the courts[2] or as a means of beginning to introduce peaceful conflict resolution in the countries emerging from war, and which now have to rebuild their systems of justice from scratch. This requires the always lengthy process of training judges and an infrastructure that is not always among the priorities of immediate international aid. Mediation may therefore appear to be a convenient way of adapting to realities on the ground. In the framework of the Stability Pact for South Eastern Europe, a multilateral seminar on alternative methods of settling disputes was organised in 1999. The seminar's priorities were commercial and civil questions but an extension to other fields is planned. The Council of Europe has given the Committee of Experts on the Efficiency of Justice terms of reference to work on the question of mediation. The Committee of Ministers recommended an extension to administrative disputes in 2001.[3]

The Tampere Declaration recalls that justice must be seen as a means of facilitat-ing the daily life of citizens through better access to justice that entails setting up alternative means of settling disputes.[4] The varied expectations of institutional leaders are clear but are not necessarily translated into initiatives on the ground or reflected in the national policies of some countries.

The example of the Thames Valley Police in the United Kingdom, which intro-duced the principle of restorative justice into the legal system, shows the scale the new policy can have. The system of cautioning by the police, a legal mechanism whereby the police do not have to send cases to the prosecutor, was applied to one-third of cases in 2001, and Thames Valley Police decided to use it to organise a meeting with the victim in the presence of specially trained police officers. Some earlier research had shown that the police often used the procedure in order to

---

1. European Forum for Victim-Offender Mediation: Making Restorative Justice Work, 27-29 October 1999, Louvain, Belgium.
2. Committee of Ministers Recommendation No. R (1999) 19 concerning mediation in penal matters, Council of Europe.
3. Committee of Ministers Recommendation No. R (2001) 9 on alternatives to litigation between administrative authorities and private parties, Council of Europe.
4. European Council on the creation of an area of freedom, security and justice, Tampere 15-16 October 1999, European Union: Bulletin EU 5-2002.

humiliate and frighten the person. In 1998, it was decided to transform procedure with respect to adults and minors. Almost 600 "restorative conferences" are held each year, representing two-thirds of cautioning procedures. Researchers have noted the positive impact on re-offending rates.[1]

An act on mediation passed in Norway on 15 March 1991 enables any citizen to take a case of any kind to a mediator. This is an important principle since it frees citizens of the ordeal of taking their cases into the administrative, criminal or civil systems, which is the main obstacle to citizens' access to justice. The police and the prosecutor are able to refer cases to a mediator. This is therefore an alternative to standard criminal proceedings. Initially, cases were of limited gravity, but the Norwegian parliament is planning to raise the threshold and apply mediation to more serious cases of violence.

Forty mediation centres have therefore been established, some of which, like the one in Oslo, employ a number of people and over a hundred voluntary mediators who are given training, paid expenses and come from different professions and walks of life. The mediation service is free and every city must provide and fund such a service. This ensures equality of access to mediation.

In 2001, the centres dealt with 6 500 cases, most of which concerned juveniles of 15 to 17 involved in vandalism or theft. Most of the agreements reached between parties were for financial compensation and repair work. Failure to comply with the agreement recorded by the mediator may lead to court proceedings. The main obstacle to the development of such services appears to be the extent of local authority involvement and participation in discussions; the other obstacle is a certain lack of interest on the part of the police.

France, possibly less systematically, is beginning to develop mediation services. On the basis of the power of public prosecutors to send cases referred to them to mediation, voluntary bodies or individuals gradually trained and authorised to do the work provide the service, particularly with the co-operation of towns and cities. The service is frequently provided by the law and justice centres or, if not, by community structures. Other forms of mediation are being developed with respect to the family and citizens' relations with government departments. There is as yet no common doctrine uniting all these initiatives, notably with respect to the nature of their relationship with the local social fabric, so restorative justice is not always satisfied in all its dimensions.

United Kingdom also has a civil society movement seeking to set up community mediation centres which are in most cases funded by local authorities. They give individuals the opportunity to find a neutral place in which to express their feelings, fears and aggression. Most cases are referred to them by the police or social workers and concern family disputes or disputes between neighbours. So far, more than 150 centres have been opened.

---

1. Richard Young and Carolyn Hoyle, *An evaluation of the implementation and effectiveness of an initiative in restorative cautioning,* Oxford University, May 2002.

The women's movement and its fight against violence have given birth to a large number of mediation centres, although a section of the movement has always considered that the seriousness of the offences excluded this form of justice and required traditional justice and imprisonment. The weakness of such specialised centres is that they are too dependent on the parties' agreeing to go to them. In addition, their involvement in community-based work is extremely variable. However, the firm commitment of professions, such as prosecutors and the police, undeniably gives the process credibility in the eyes of the community.

It should also be remembered that mediation in criminal cases has to respect the European standards laid down in Article 6 of the European Convention on Human Rights. A recommendation of the Committee of Ministers recalls some of its principles: respect of the rights of the defence, full understanding by the parties of the nature of the case, requirement that juveniles be assisted by their parents.[1]

The Créteil Conference on Mediation, organised during the French presidency of the European Union, gave a clearer idea of the different forms of mediation, such as judicial, social, by agreement and so forth, that are flourishing in Europe.[2] Professor Duccio Scatolero, professor of criminology at the University of Turin (Italy), situated the mediation process in the context of the city, with the problems presented by the coexistence of several cultural models. According to him, mediation concerned the civilisation of the urban territory. What was new was the discovery of a "spirit" of mediation, in other words, the mediator's ability to look at a number of aspects of the same problem. He added that we should go from "mediation of disputes to mediation of differences". Can these two types of mediation, of disputes and differences, be defined more clearly?

At this conference, Erik Winnerstrom, from the Swedish Ministry of Justice, attempted to provide a typology. According to him, if a comparison were made between traditional mediation and social mediation, it would be found that the former intervenes once tensions have reached the point of open conflict, while the latter intervenes at an earlier stage and therefore covers a series of events from the causes at the root of problems to conflict management, by way of conflict reduction. He described social mediation as a way of empowering the positive individual components of society so as to encourage them to take responsibility for maintaining social harmony and preventing crime. Giving such scope to mediation enables us to identify more clearly what we might call "the mediation of disputes".

However, there is no fundamental difference in the practice of these forms of mediation. The aim is always, with the mediator's help, to put the complexity, the rich emotional and psychological background and the social and economic context of the problem into words. This process is also at the heart of living democracy, a

---

1. Committee of Ministers Recommendation No. R (1999) 19 concerning mediation in penal matters, Council of Europe.
2. *Nouveaux modes de résolution des conflits de la vie quotidienne* (based on Créteil conference: Médiation sociale et nouveaux modes de résolution des conflits de la vie quotidienne, organised by the Délégation interministérielle à la Ville and the European Commission, 21-23 September 2000) Collection : Rencontres des acteurs de la ville, Editions de la DIV, France.

point made, in different terms, by a Brussels mediator working on relations between the police and young Moroccans: "learning to express one's thoughts and feelings in every situation boils down to learning how to live with different opinions, and there we have the whole philosophy of life in society".

This social-life philosophy is producing a large number of initiatives, particularly to help groups with integration difficulties and which suffer from particular disadvantages. They are at work in the most unexpected fields, the public spaces of our cities, sports grounds, mass entertainment events, health care premises, and in relations between governors and governed to name but some.

France has put in place 300 delegates of the Mediator of the Republic in disadvantaged neighbourhoods in an attempt to "reduce the inhabitants' feelings of injustice with respect to public services". Young people from immigrant families are particularly vulnerable to these types of feelings when they suffer discrimination. The delegates see individuals, make reports on the various services and take part in discussions on reform of the working practices of public servants.

Mediators have been introduced in a number of countries to enter into contact with potentially violent groups of supporters and work with them on an on-going basis to deflect violence and transform it into actions that are positive for the people involved and the community, on the model of the "fan coaching"[1] developed by the city of Liège in Belgium.

Again, in Italian cities with high levels of prostitution, mediators intervene to resolve the demands of local people living near places of prostitution.

Some cities situated on routes followed by Roma/Gypsies are putting mediators in place to iron out the problems of encampments and relations with local people. It is interesting to note a CLRAE resolution[2] encouraging Roma/Gypsies to provide information about their cultural identity to other communities and organise themselves to gain acceptance by local authorities as partners.

Many public services in Europe have, under various names, established services specialising in receiving the public and above all preventing risks of conflict with users. This can be seen as a way of managing the inadequacies of services and avoiding reforming them, which amounts to ignoring the many sociological studies showing that the ways institutions function can always generate what users experience as violence and is likely to generate a reaction or violence in return. Railway companies, in particular, have done a great deal of work on this issue.

It is undeniable that the functions of mediation in public spaces indirectly operate a sort of watch, a new social control, on those spaces, while experts cite the disappearance or weakness of traditional modes of social control as one of the causes of urban insecurity.

---

1. See: http://www.eurofan.org and *The prevention of violence in sport,* Council of Europe Publishing, 2002.
2. CLRAE Resolution 249 (1993) on Gypsies in Europe: the role and responsibility of local and regional authorities, Council of Europe.

The realism of restorative justice

The enormous restorative justice movement gives rise to a great many questions as to its relevance and the methods of introducing it into legal systems. An initial question is whether it supplements or is an alternative to the criminal justice system. We have seen that the discussion in the Committee of Ministers[1] saw the system as a means of alleviating the material burden on systems and also as an advantage for individuals in terms of the quality of decisions. But would it not be preferable to see the system first as an improvement for people charged with offences, and in this respect, as alternative rather than supplementary? It is an issue concerning justice that we now have to tackle in which the relationship of trust between citizens and democracy is at stake. European ministers of justice should establish in their organisation charts departments that give impetus to the implementation of such programmes.

Can restorative justice be applied to all criminal law offences as well as to offences governed by other areas of law, such as civil law, social law and commercial law? Theoretically, the method can be applied to all criminal offences. It is clear, however, that the question depends, not on any technical difficulty in its implementation, but rather on a political difficulty: can the state accept that offences affecting its essential interests should be dealt with in this way? Can public opinion accept that serious offences against the person should come under it? No. Work is therefore required on how matters can be divided between the two systems of justice, bearing in mind that the dividing-line is subject to revision. The Norwegian parliament will shortly be doing this in order to extend the scope of restorative justice; the practices of prosecutors and police in Belgium, France and the United Kingdom are already very varied, surprisingly so in some people's opinion. In addition to political difficulties, there may also be less tangible obstacles such as those concerning sexual questions within the family. Psychological problems are perhaps better dealt with by traditional ways of comforting victims and helping them overcome the trauma they have suffered. Nothing is impossible, however.

Justice without constraints

Lastly, can restorative justice be based on constraint? Freely accepted constraint? Asking this question involves separating it from the question of prison. In the framework of restorative justice, the process between the three parties – offender, victim and community – ends with the acceptance of duties to be fulfilled (duties to perform) or prohibitions that have to be respected (orders not to do). The distress caused to the victim and the community may necessitate positive measures, freely accepted by the individual, such as paying, compensating, refraining, to name a few. Such measures can obviously only do without the power of a court if the violation of freedom is not too great, according to thresholds that remain to be determined (prison is of course completely excluded from such measures).

---

1. Committee of Ministers Recommendation No. R (1999) 19 concerning mediation in penal matters, Council of Europe.

Can restorative justice be based on the prospect of prison? Some experts do not believe prison is the first resort here but may be imposed when the undertaking given to the victim or the community is not kept. Others, in particular the promoters of the very well-known system of restorative justice in Yukon, Canada, reply that a system of justice that has the resource of prison at its disposal is justice as we now know it – a lazy system making little effort to find the best means of re-forging the social bond.

European countries could explore ways and means of organising two types of justice: One, the most commonly used, restorative justice or justice based upon dialogue, would be that of our daily life. The other would be for the exceptional, for serious crimes, requiring a symbolic use of the State, and where offenders may be imprisoned.

V. THE GOVERNANCE OF VIOLENCE

We are in a period in which the response to violence and insecurity is neither one thing nor the other: we have criminal justice systems that are trying to find their way and dare not unequivocally commit themselves to restorative justice, public policies in various states of imbalance as a result of budgetary redeployment, governments searching for legitimacy in the face of the development of personal involvement, the ascendancy of European laws not explained to citizens and the development of individuality. This individuality is taking the form of an often aggressive individualism seeking instant gratification. We need to find other ways of governing the nation and the public good that is security.

This is what is at stake in urban governance. The concept of governance is complex and controversial. It comes from the financial and economic world, and the World Bank has used it a great deal in order to impose structural adjustment on developing countries, a policy now generally questioned. It has left behind a managerial approach to government, but above all the conviction that power also exists outside the sphere of formal government authority.

According to the United Nations,[1] governance is an efficient and effective response to urban problems by local authorities, which are accountable for their actions and act in partnership with civil society. It is based on a change in the direct supply of goods and services by the government towards an approach which delegates responsibility, characterised by three principal strategies: decentralisation of responsibilities and resources to local authorities, encouraging participation in civil society, and the creation of partnerships for the purposes of achieving common objectives. The notion of responsibility is central: initiatives must be linked to the democratic authority as a guarantor of the common good and respect for rights and the law. From this point of view, local government is in a pivotal position, if it has sufficient resources and authority.

Interdependence

Present modes of government in Europe aim at decentralised decision-making accompanied by distribution of decision-making. This trend is ineluctably leading to the development of levels of government particular to each of the issues dealt with. Jurisdiction is divided according to the rule of subsidiarity: from the local to the international, by way of the regional, national and European levels – jurisdiction lies with the lowest level best able to respond to a particular problem. This

---

1. Global Campaign for Good Urban Governance, United Nations Human Settlements Programme (UN Habitat) (see http://www.unchs.org/).

rule implies developing dialogue between the different levels of government, and transparency to enable citizens to monitor decision-making.

Security and crime prevention are not escaping decentralisation and therefore distribution between levels of government. Three factors argue in favour of constant involvement of supra-local levels of government in new prevention and security policies.

First, there is a risk that national security policies (favouring use of the criminal law) will be inconsistent with local security policies (more geared towards risk management and new prevention measures); the result of such a split would be the juxtaposition of new preventive measures and traditional forms of social control.

Second, the proximity, even of the local authority, could become unbearable without the possibility of having recourse to other levels of expertise and support and to national law, or even supranational law, such as the European Convention on Human Rights, and, in general, to bodies other than local ones.

Last, the interdependence of territories requires regulatory and compensatory action among them, the organisation of flows of ideas, goods and human beings.

Local coalitions

Dialogue between the different levels of government requires some stability and therefore presupposes a framework. Coalitions have been formed at local level which propel and structure new forms of co-operation between government bodies and economic and social players. The majority of European countries are now trying to formalise co-operative strategies in the service of local security policies; contracts, agreements and protocols are being concluded between the different levels of government. In the United Kingdom, local authorities and the police are the prime movers in setting-up a "community safety strategy" for three-year periods. In Italy, protocols of agreement have been signed between prefectures and cities for two-year periods. In Belgium, the first security contracts were signed in 1992 and have become security and society contracts. Security contracts have also been set up in France by local security and prevention councils. Since 1999, Germany has had local prevention councils. Lithuania has put in place agreements between cities and government involving the Ministry of Education, NGOs and quite a large number of private security companies. Slovak Republic is implementing the same type of approach at regional level and in programmes set up in the framework of the Crime Prevention Strategy of the Slovak Republic.

Coalitions that stimulate projects

Coalitions should make it possible to stimulate civil society and communities to develop initiatives and give them the opportunity of prospering and perhaps taking over some public actions or offsetting the inadequacy of public measures. Every day, schools, transport companies, social backers, shopkeepers, cultural and sports facility managers, town-planners and architects, service companies, industries and so forth, are participating in different ways in the local evaluation of security, financing prevention and integration projects, providing job opportunities, providing informal security in public spaces, designing safer, more reassuring places and playing the role of mediators, to name a few examples. Some take part in local prevention and security coalitions under the aegis of the local authorities, either individually or through their professional organisations, such as chambers of commerce and industry. This results in their initiatives being better co-ordinated, consistent and mutually enriching. They are now more closely linked to the public supply of security. Participation of this type by private sector companies often takes place at national level.

Germany, for example, has created a prevention forum bringing together major German insurance companies, major distribution and electronics chains. The Dutch Government is to create a foundation linking state and private sector. The national prevention programmes in the United Kingdom and Canada (Business in the Community) include company intervention programmes which, for example, enable company executives to go into schools in order to bring their expertise to disadvantaged children.

Because it provides services, the commercial security sector is involved minimally in coalitions, but linkage between the public and private supply of security is increasingly mentioned in cities. Partnerships are developing for the management of major events, public spaces, the interface between semi-public and public spaces, the security of public buildings and the development of targeted security in cities.[1]

It is perhaps a little less a partnership of weakness (joining forces instead of reforming) and more a partnership that is reorganising community services so as to make people's lives easier, alleviate tension, resolve problems – in short, to produce the common good.

This is a crucial stage. We should take the initiative and not allow deregulation to dislocate our cities. We should create social inclusion. Security, yes, but security that strengthens the pluralism, vitality and complexity of our cities. We should make the initiatives of civil society, institutional mechanisms and the use of the commercial security sector part of a participatory democratic process. We must democratise access to security, freedom and justice. The future of our cities depends upon the co-ordination of the roles and responsibilities we entrust to public authorities, civil society and commercial interests for applying the law, exercising constraint, remedying violence and violations of individual rights and freedoms, and renewing public space.

Cities and the management of violence

Urban security has become one of the central issues of cities, along with culture, the environment and health. Security is seen as essential to cities and their

---

1. *Plus de sécurité dans l'environnement,* Secrétariat Permanent à la Politique de Prévention, Belgium, 1994.

renewal, an element in their identity and the competition between them and between urban projects.

The common good

Society's preoccupation with violence and insecurity perhaps specifically invites us to re-examine what causes tension, inequality, contradictions and dichotomies in our cities. How do rich and poor, young people and adults, men and women, indigenous people and immigrants, the sedentary and the nomadic, the life of day and the life of night, standards and the law, coexist today? Asking the question is to disrupt urban projects (renewal, construction, planning) which are still finding it difficult to take into account and therefore anticipate conflict. Too many projects are conceived in a vacuum, do not include any social impact study, approach security only in technical terms confined to buildings (such as stability, fire), do not recognise the inter-relatedness of the spaces to which they are linked. Not raising the issue of conflict in urban planning and management is to opt for an imaginary consensus and create public spaces incapable of making visible and embracing the contradictions of the city.[1]

Conversely, we need to combat the autonomisation of crime prevention. By confining ourselves to an extremely technical approach to the question of crime, we run the risk of constructing a totalitarian security policy favouring certain interests. Like health and education, security is a common good and should therefore be subject to rules of equitable distribution. It is extremely worrying to note the great influence of crime prevention, rather than the prevention of poverty, for example, in urban policies, and this may result in social policy being redefined solely according to its effects on crime.[2] Security is part of sustainable development policy.

This new mode of government has no meaning unless there is a close relationship with citizens, and it is the cities, where most of the population of Europe is concentrated, that provide the framework for the application and accomplishment of this method. According to the principle of subsidiarity, cities are the principal actors in the reduction of insecurity. The European Commission's "Sustainable urban development in the European Union: a framework for action" sets "contributing to good urban governance and local empowerment" as an objective for European policies. The document goes on to favour "innovative urban development strategies aimed at promoting good urban governance, empowerment and urban security ... Towns and cities can play an important role in meeting the objectives enshrined in the Treaty".[3]

---

1. Jordi Borja and Zaida Muxi, *L'espai públic: ciudad i ciutadania,* Diputació de Barcelona, February 2002.
2. Adam Crawford (Centre for Criminal Justice Studies, University of Leeds, UK), "The present and future governance of urban security" – presentation to the European Forum for Urban Security Conference, Naples, December 2000.
3. "Sustainable urban development in the European Union: a framework for action", communication from the European Commission to the Council of Europe, the European Parliament, the Economic and Social Committee and the Committee of the Regions, 25 May 1999.

Cities are defending this role by developing a policy of co-operation on the national and international scenes and, at local level, a policy of joint production of security.

The role of the local political authority

The local political authority has a decisive role to play: it stands at the intersection of different technical capabilities, is responsible for the integrity of the municipal territory, is able to negotiate with other levels of government and is in the front line as regards accountability to the electorate for the quality of the city. Local authorities are principally responsible for introducing and guiding the participatory process since they are in a better position to synthesise, in the name of the people who have elected them, and are in any case able to speak to all the parties involved in the process.

The police, like the judiciary, may be a driving force in community participation, in particular prevention measures, but it is up to the local authority to set up clear links between city level and proximity or community levels, especially where there are conflicts of interest. It is also responsible for including measures specific to a more comprehensive social and economic development policy.

Local authorities are responsible for:

– putting in place ways of enabling inhabitants,[1] including the most marginalised, to contribute to the decision-making processes that affect their lives and gain access to social and political participation. Inhabitants may participate in many ways, but it has to be recognised that most forms of participation are addressed to those with a minimum of knowledge of local life and its institutions. People involved in integration programmes are the last to be put in a position to participate. Several times in the last ten years the Council of Europe has stressed the need to involve young people in public life, since it is worried that young people are becoming disaffected.[2] In 2002, this Organisation stressed the urgent need to help young people who find it difficult to participate to become active citizens, in particular to avoid negative phenomena such as exclusion and destructive forms of behaviour such as violence and drug-taking which may marginalise them. It went on to say that early participation gave better knowledge of society and a feeling of belonging. It was highly desirable to push back urban insecurity, form associations for implementing projects to combat violence and promote tolerance both within and outside schools. The CLRAE is planning to revise the European

---

1. International Decade for the Culture of Peace and Non-violence for the Children of the World, 2000-10, 6th Programme on Democratic Participation, Unesco.
2. Committee of Ministers Recommendation No. R (1997) 3 on youth participation and the future of civil society, Council of Europe.
3. CLRAE 4th Conference on Youth: Actors in their Cities and Regions, Cracow, 7-8 March 2002, Council of Europe.

Charter on Youth Participation, in particular to encourage cities to develop youth councils:[3]

– ensuring that the participatory and partnership process does not develop to the detriment of a group or territory. Many cities have poor neighbourhoods where living conditions are particularly bad and people feel little able to influence their way of life. Such neighbourhoods suffer discrimination in terms of the nature of the services and facilities with which they are provided; the authorities often refuse to give them a new underground line; the young people who live there are rejected by the job market. Such mistrust on the part of the city rebounds on the inhabitants of the neighbourhood who feel still more disadvantaged;

– taking into account the necessary renewal of professions at work in the governance of urban security.[1] Two new capabilities are being developed in cities, the community-based approach and the local management of governance. In places the provision of certain urban security services is delegated, often in innovative ways, to persons who intervene outside the traditional field of activity of police and judiciary. Their function may be to facilitate access to the law and the application of the law in daily life, to guarantee the security of people and spaces, settle disputes, maintain and promote equality in the use of public space, maintain the quality of that space and prevent it being wilfully damaged, and help to manage exceptional uses of the space. Cities now recognise the need for them to be professionalised and this is starting to happen;[2]

– opening and running new arenas for decision-making on security problems and linking them to the local coalition. Such arenas may be of different kinds, according to the geography of insecurity. No social or economic phenomenon will ever respect administrative and political boundaries, and it is the responsibility of local authorities to identify the territories specific to each issue, irrespective of jurisdiction. Cities frequently enter into inter-district co-operation, even on an informal basis, and sometimes do so at regional level, in order to solve or anticipate problems in their own territories. A local incident may have causes in the neighbouring town or beyond; security measures in one neighbourhood may have repercussions (new flows, new opportunities, new tensions) in the next town. Such inter-city solidarity may exist between cities far apart with the same sorts of problems which have at least some of the keys to the success of the actions undertaken. This is increasingly often the case with respect to the issue of Roma/Gypsy encampments and the return of runaway children.

Developing the role of cities is the essential response to the risk that distant, prescriptive modes of government imply for cities: a society looking to the market for what it does not receive from those governing it, and from the community alone the social bond it does not feel elsewhere. The commercial supply of security and purchasing power would thus shape urban space and its management and protection.

---

1. *Safety and security: new jobs for the millennium,* European Forum for Urban Security, Paris, 1997.
2. "Sécucités manager", training reference manual issued by the European Forum for Urban Security, March 2000 and "Community justice workers", Nacro training programme, UK.

This shape is that of a city widening the gap between rich and poor, a society fragmented into communities or territories closed in on themselves.

The "common good" would then be reduced to the legitimate "good for oneself" or "good for one's own". Cities must become cities of justice, security and freedom.[1] The European Union and the Council of Europe are the purveyors of these values in their fields of jurisdiction and should rely on and encourage every European city to implement them.

Constructing the collective response to violence

The other response that has to be constructed around victims and offenders is based on the strong involvement of the community, of civil society. Such a collective response can be developed only in the cities of Europe, within the everyday communities of the inhabitants of Europe. This everyday proximity is essential for diagnosing and evaluating problems and constructing reasoned responses to them. The participation of civil society has gradually asserted itself as one of the key strategies of urban security at the various levels of government responsible for crime prevention and security.

Representative democracy alone cannot resolve the problems generated by insecurity or the feeling of insecurity; participatory democracy is also needed. Professionals alone will never be able to reorganise a society in which the violence of adults becomes the violence of children and crime an alternative to poverty.

The participation of civil society in urban security policies is a response to the observation that crime, violence and drugs can no longer be regarded as temporary lapses by our societies but as symptoms of their dysfunction. It is this underlying dysfunction that has to be dealt with; in the meantime, we have to live with the symptoms. Living with the symptoms means finding a balance between risk management on the one hand and a reduction in the social nuisances linked to those risks on the other. In order to do this, a security policy will try sufficiently to recreate the bond and confidence (in oneself and others) to enable civil society to live with the symptoms and limit their violence. It is impossible to do this without the participation of the people who run the greatest risks and put up with the disruption they cause. All cities experience this on a day-to-day basis. They also experience the fact that such participation enables society to reorganise itself a little better and to some extent break the vicious circle of violence responding to violence which engenders violence in its turn.

Social control

The implementation of the principle of participation by civil society aims indirectly to revive the informal social control that once existed in cities. There is probably less delinquency in the streets of southern Europe because there are so many people on the streets and family networks remain close in neighbourhoods.

---

1. "The safety and democracy manifesto"(Naples Manifesto) 9 December 2000, European Forum for Urban Security.

But who exercises social control: society as a whole or a particular social stratum?[1] Most of the 10 million Britons involved in "neighbourhood watch" schemes are middle class. Participation by local people in France is almost exclusively in areas of social housing. In Italy, the territories where there is the greatest involvement are those that enjoy a degree of stability. The most difficult are always people experiencing a rapid transformation in the social fabric (the settlement of an immigrant group, the gradual disappearance of a once dominant working class, change in the dominant social group, the coexistence of socio-ethnic groups with differing values, cultural references and economic capability), or again outlying neighbourhoods that are even less homogeneous and generally characterised by significant urban transformation (hypermarkets, roads, railway junctions) or recently constructed residential neighbourhoods.

The question of the place of minorities, immigrants, the poorest and the most alienated (drug users, delinquents) arises in all these cases with respect to participatory processes.

Here too, the role of local authorities is decisive for reaching out to the most alienated and guaranteeing that social control does not develop to the benefit of one group and the detriment of another, and is not diverted into discriminatory security measures detrimental to the common good.

Communities, inhabitants and citizens

There is no general agreement on the definition of the community in Europe. However, the word "community" expresses the plurality of physical and symbolic proximities: it refers to people grouped on the basis of geography and/or common interest, identity or interaction. It is a notion of varying geometry and therefore perhaps richer than "inhabitants", more closely linked to territory. It makes it possible to escape the spatial confinement to which the notion of proximity all too easily gives rise. The word "citizens", also used because it refers to, in particular, political rights and duties, has the disadvantage of being linked to nationality, and therefore excludes foreign residents. Since the 10th UN congress on crime, the term *"collectivité"* has also been used.[2]

Is there one Europe mainly organised on the basis of community, specificity and particularism, and another organised on the basis of citizenship, national unity and integration?

Dialogues are beginning, there is some harmonisation and mutual enrichment thanks to recognition on both sides. The first is the recognition by the English-speaking countries themselves of a risk (inherent in a community approach) of social fragmentation, individual or group isolation, a *de facto* privatisation of public space. At the same time, there is greater recognition of the risk (inherent in an integrationist approach) of denying to the different constituents of a nation the

---

1. Stanley Cohen, *Visions of social control, punishment and classification*, Polity Press, Cambridge, 1985.
2. "Community involvement in crime prevention", background paper for the 10th UN Congress on the Prevention of Crime and the Treatment of Offenders (10-17 April 2000, Vienna), United Nations.

desire for group identity and the ability to defend their space or group when threatened by violence, drugs and delinquency.

Another recognition, finally: it is now clear that forms of participation are developing essentially in the middle classes, with a real risk of discrimination in access to security, the poorer classes having no real access to the police or to modes of organisation that are more appropriate to more favourable socio-economic contexts. This has led cities to diversify channels of access to civil society so as to get closer to the problems of the poor.

The opportunities for mobilisation

Generally speaking, there are two possible scenarios for cities. The first is more reactive and selective and will be born on the initiative either of civil society (inhabitants, NGOs, service companies, and so forth) or the authorities. There is participation in response to a particular incident or in order to have a certain measure adopted. Participation then continues after the initial event and is extended to other places or profoundly changes the approach of local authorities and their partners to security problems. We have seen this scenario played out with respect to street prostitution, young beggars and violence against children. It may lead to excesses of security and violations of freedoms if elected or institutional officials do not co-operate.

The second scenario introduces participation as a way of governing security.[1] The aim is to seek consensus, or at least establish minimum rules, for organising debate in a field where rumour, anxiety, tension, even violence, play an important role.

The objectives of the participation policy

A comparison of the different scenarios of community involvement in European cities shows there to be different motivations. Some try to organise a weakened community, others to defend it against an external danger.

The social reorganisation of a vulnerable community. When vulnerability is internal to a community (too poor, too distant, too discriminated against or traumatised, etc.), the authorities may give it the necessary resources and improve residents' overall living conditions. The relations between the institutions from which the resources come and voluntary groups (such as neighbourhood committees, local associations, consumers' groups) play an important role. An attempt is made to consolidate institutions and the community structure: strengthening standards of conduct and values, assisting the socialisation of young people, mobilising internal and external resources, resisting frustrations resulting from poverty and lack of economic and social opportunity. Reducing crime and the feeling of insecurity are indirect objectives of such consolidation.[2]

---

1. D. Sansfaçon and B. Welsh, *Crime Prevention Digest II. Comparative analysis of successful community safety,* International Centre for the Prevention of Crime, Montreal, 1999.
2. J. Reiss and J. A. Roth, *Understanding and preventing violence,* online publication (see: http://www.nap.edu/browse.html) National Academies Press, 1993.

Defending the community. The starting-point here is fear and the perception of insecurity; the community's vulnerability is attributed to the fact of being "penetrable" by external elements.[1] The objectives of crime prevention and reducing opportunities for crime are more direct here. Attention is focused on the victims, rather than the authors, of offences. An attempt is made to strengthen residents' identity and their feeling of security in symbolic rather than structural terms. Protecting actual or potential victims is central and citizens take responsibility for their own security. A strategy with a direct effect on security is favoured: in most cases an *ad hoc* group is formed to watch private spaces (the neighbourhood, the building) and also the public space surrounding it, for example, a park or an area of relaxation and transition within the neighbourhood. The strategy may therefore also have the indirect, symbolic effect of privatising public spaces by establishing the principle that the order that should reign in the public space adjacent to a private space is that of the residents and not of other users. The most frequently used strategies in this second approach are the different kinds of security entrusted to community groups (neighbourhood watch, for example). Such strategies are characterised by significant intervention by institutions in the community which is asked to observe and report.

The distinction between the two approaches to participation is largely a matter of the identity of the authority that initiates and guides participation. The Europe in which the police exercise leadership and targeted prevention is firmly established, has developed a community defence strategy. In the Europe in which the main actors in prevention policies are local actors other than the police, the strategies that mobilise communities are consistent with the capabilities of those local actors (neighbourhood rehabilitation, social and cultural revitalisation of public spaces and so forth) and citizens' involvement in security is sporadic.

Such contrasts are perhaps disappearing, however: the former is adopting social development strategies first introduced in France, then Belgium, adding method to them (such as monitoring and evaluation), while the latter is paying renewed attention to targeted prevention, a type of prevention concerning the protection of targets of offences.

---

1. *Local participation in strategies for the prevention and control of drug abuse,* European Forum for Urban Security, June 1998 collection.

VI. A WORLD OF VIOLENCE

We are at war, not only at war against drugs, crime, violence, terrorism, "evil" empires and rogue states, but for our development. The countries of southern Europe learned this when they tried to gain access to our markets for their agricultural products. Our language is the language of war; we are reconstructing our state apparatuses around identified dangers, both internal and external.[1]

Freedom and security

The law is trembling; assailed by internal demands to create instruments for an implacable fight against crime and violence, pressured by the international order of the fight against terrorism, our freedoms have entered into a grey area. Controls, detection, files, finger-prints, frisking, searches, prolonged detention, anonymous testimony, internment, prison for juveniles, extradition, all these are now on parliamentary agendas. By the grace of democracy, the courts are there to judge the lawfulness of such restrictions. Is this enough to allow us to hope serenely for the development of our freedoms? It is this issue that underlies the decision of the Supreme Court of Israel on orders issued to the families of suicide bombers to move to another part of the Palestinian Territory. The situations we are experiencing in Europe are not comparable, but the Israeli judges, in an extreme situation, have given us some of the answers we have been looking for.

> The state seeks to act within the framework of the lawful possibilities available to it under the international law to which it is subject and in accordance with its internal law. As a result, not every effective measure is also a lawful measure. Also our role as judges is not easy. We are doing all we can to balance properly between human rights and the security of the area. In this balance, human rights cannot receive complete protection, as if there were no terror, and State security cannot receive complete protection, as if there were no human rights. A delicate and sensitive balance is required. This is the price of democracy. It is expensive, but worthwhile. It strengthens the state. It provides a reason for its struggle. Our work, as judges, is hard. *(From a decision of the Supreme Court of Israel, 3 September 2002)*

The delicate, sensitive balance the judges were looking for has created some strange legal concepts, the vagueness of which may lead them to be applied across the legal spectrum, including in domestic law. The judges draw a distinction between "imperative reasons of security" and "imperative military reasons". This shows us that the traditional outlines of the organisation of our states are being challenged by the issue of security. In the context of this security policy, the only

---

1. The Dutch Ministry of the Interior's Public Safety and Security programme brings together the agencies providing prevention services in cities, the police, an agency that deals with national disasters, the fire service, the technological communication services and the national security services.

relevant criterion for judging the lawfulness of a government decision is the "zone of reasonableness".

It is for each one of us to decide what is reasonable in relation to our own situation. The Council of Europe has evaluated this "reasonableness" by adopting international *Guidelines of the Committee of Ministers of the Council of Europe on human rights and the fight against terrorism.*[1]

The globalisation of violence – terrorists living in the neighbourhoods of our cities and being educated in our schools and universities – has us by the throat. The violence we wish to eradicate is born of human misery, a striking contradiction which should lead us to examine our past and our present.

The globalisation of domestic and community violence, the violence of others and of cities and states has called into question the traditional distinction between internal order and the international order. The world market of violence is becoming a single market in which the products are very different, but are directly linked. Our feeling of insecurity is fuelled by this globalisation. Apart from this rather pessimistic observation which casts doubt on our ability to act to reduce tense atmospheres, the international order can teach us a few ways of reducing conflict and tackling violence.

Lessons of the international order

The international order takes us into a complex world of negotiating tables and mediation, sometimes disrupted by outbreaks of war, but old enough to have laid down a corpus of tenets and smooth-running methods.

Since the establishment of the League of Nations in Geneva, there has been a proliferation of legal instruments and diplomatic mechanisms that aim to prevent and control conflict. Innumerable international organisations and regular conferences bring states together in every domain perceived as a potential generator of conflict. Everyone hopes that international economic development without borders and with no regulatory obstacles will be able to bring peace and pacify spirits. This is Adam Smith's old formula on the development of commercial exchange as peaceful trade. The term is understood in the sense of an ambient civility, understanding, trade against violence. "Reform of foreign police forces was widely recognised as necessary to support the expansion of democracy and to ensure a safe environment abroad for market economies".[2] This civilisation of trade requires a proliferation of conflict resolution bodies.

The international sphere has all the tools of conflict resolution. Arbitration is commonly used in a number of domains, as is conciliation; mediation is carried out by international authorities and enshrined in political declarations establishing regional bodies, such as the new Organisation for African Unity and the Stability

---

1. Council of Europe Publishing, 2002.
2. David H. Bayley, *Democratizing the police abroad: what to do and how to do it,* US Department of Justice – National Institute of Justice, 2001.

Pact for South Eastern Europe. To this panoply have been added international courts, first in the commercial field, then in the field of human rights.

These courts have been joined by armed forces under the aegis of the United Nations that place themselves between the belligerents, through missions ranging from simple presence to armed intervention. Then an embryonic international police force began to be formed: in February 2000, the United Nations had at its disposal a corps of 9 000 civilian police officers from 34 countries whose mission was to train local police but also to enforce order and place themselves at the disposal of the new international courts, notably in Kosovo and Timor.[1] The United States has been playing a major role in this development. President Clinton entrusted the State Department with the task of co-ordinating the US agencies involved and building partnerships with the Justice Department so that judicial and penal systems could be established during peace operations. This American priority was strengthened by the events of 11 September 2001.

The Council of Europe has also felt the need to give coherence to European interventions and has set up a council for police matters to "contribute to a closer co-operation between ministries of justice and interior, prosecution, police, internal security services and their subordinate structures".[2] The European Union is certainly the most advanced model of this international order, part of whose mission is to avoid violence by imposing peace-keeping forces.

Violence in the world has its instruments of containment and reduction; the internal violence of our cities and countries is still looking for a renewal of their instruments. Restorative justice seems to be the type of justice most appropriate to our multicultural societies open to the world and to all the dangers of that world.

What, then, is security today?

The organisation charts of all European ministries of the interior give a picture of the integration of every danger within a single entity, whose reactive measures are, in the final analysis, drawn from the same source and differ only in their degree of gravity. Internal and external security are one and the same. This merger makes for greater effectiveness – we will see if that is so later.

In the last ten years, the concept of security has been refined by taking more account of social perceptions and victims' experiences and the development of risk reduction policies. Crime, pollution, fire, violence on the roads and health risks are references. A problem that emerges in one of these fields (following a chance event or a strategy) sometimes finds a solution in another field, as is clearly shown in a survey of the work of various Council of Europe bodies.[3] For example,

---

1. Ibid.
2. Conference of Ministers of the Interior: Police of the 21st Century: Strengthening the Protection of Citizens' Rights and New International Threats against Security (Bucharest, 22-23 June 2000), Council of Europe.
3. "Survey of key texts by the Council of Europe in connection with violence and urban security", (forthcoming document) integrated project "Responses to violence in everyday life in a democratic society", Council of Europe.

some crime problems find solutions in the field of public health or management of a space and vice versa. However, the organising authority with formal jurisdiction or the one to which the problem is first referred still largely determines the outcome. The possibilities for linkage between the various fields of security could be better exploited and the passage from one field to another made smoother.

The dual international movement of human rights and reconsideration of economic development in terms of its negative impact on humanity is dominating international reflection and has led to the emergence of the concept of integrated personal development, which does not necessarily coincide with the development of countries.[1] In addition to human rights, the individual should have a right to complete security, "human security". This "human security" places individuals in their environment and assesses their vulnerability. One can speak in terms of an ecology of security. Vicenç Fisas does not see the concept of "human security" in this way but he does recognise that it has the merit of forcing the globalisation of various issues, from antipersonnel mines to police violence, by way of sexual harassment. An ecology of security? Security as a preliminary to sustainable development or, more modestly, the "basic requirements for a successful society with a decent quality of life"?[2]

To conclude, a question

On every beach in the world, groups of children are having fun by burying one of their number in the sand amid showers of water and gales of laughter. Every one these groups always has an adult with them, shouting themselves hoarse trying to forbid such games.

Question: should a second adult be put on the beach or should the children be educated? This is how the world is organised.

---

1. Vicenç Fisas "Rethinking security", *El Pais*, 1 August 2002.
2. Definition given by the Dutch Ministry of the Interior.

PUBLICATIONS BY THE INTEGRATED PROJECT "RESPONSES TO VIOLENCE IN EVERYDAY LIFE IN A DEMOCRATIC SOCIETY"

Urban crime prevention – a guide for local authorities (2002)
ISBN 92-871-4943-7

The prevention of violence in sport (2002)
ISBN 92-871-5038-9

Facets of interculturality in education (2003)
ISBN 92-871-5088-5

Towards a migration management strategy (2003)

"Response to violence in everyday life in a democratic society"
http://www.coe.int/violence

Sales agents for publications of the Council of Europe
Agents de vente des publications du Conseil de l'Europe

AUSTRALIA/AUSTRALIE
Hunter Publications, 58A, Gipps Street
AUS-3066 COLLINGWOOD, Victoria
Tel.: (61) 3 9417 5361
Fax: (61) 3 9419 7154
E-mail: Sales@hunter-pubs.com.au
http://www.hunter-pubs.com.au

BELGIUM/BELGIQUE
La Librairie européenne SA
50, avenue A. Jonnart
B-1200 BRUXELLES 20
Tel.: (32) 2 734 0281
Fax: (32) 2 735 0860
E-mail: info@libeurop.be
http://www.libeurop.be

Jean de Lannoy
202, avenue du Roi
B-1190 BRUXELLES
Tel.: (32) 2 538 4308
Fax: (32) 2 538 0841
E-mail: jean.de.lannoy@euronet.be
http://www.jean-de-lannoy.be

CANADA
Renouf Publishing Company Limited
5369 Chemin Canotek Road
CDN-OTTAWA, Ontario, K1J 9J3
Tel.: (1) 613 745 2665
Fax: (1) 613 745 7660
E-mail: order.dept@renoufbooks.com
http://www.renoufbooks.com

CZECH REPUBLIC/
RÉPUBLIQUE TCHÈQUE
Suweco Cz Dovoz Tisku Praha
Ceskomoravska 21
CZ-18021 PRAHA 9
Tel.: (420) 2 660 35 364
Fax: (420) 2 683 30 42
E-mail: import@suweco.cz

DENMARK/DANEMARK
GAD Direct
Fiolstaede 31-33
DK-1171 COPENHAGEN K
Tel.: (45) 33 13 72 33
Fax: (45) 33 12 54 94
E-mail: info@gaddirect.dk

FINLAND/FINLANDE
Akateeminen Kirjakauppa
Keskuskatu 1, PO Box 218
FIN-00381 HELSINKI
Tel.: (358) 9 121 41
Fax: (358) 9 121 4450
E-mail: akatilaus@stockmann.fi
http://www.akatilaus.akateeminen.com

FRANCE
La Documentation française
(Diffusion/Vente France entière)
124, rue H. Barbusse
F-93308 AUBERVILLIERS Cedex
Tel.: (33) 01 40 15 70 00
Fax: (33) 01 40 15 68 00
E-mail: commandes.vel@ladocfrancaise.gouv.fr
http://www.ladocfrancaise.gouv.fr

Librairie Kléber (Vente Strasbourg)
Palais de l'Europe
F-67075 STRASBOURG Cedex
Fax: (33) 03 88 52 91 21
E-mail: librairie.kleber@coe.int

GERMANY/ALLEMAGNE
AUSTRIA/AUTRICHE
UNO Verlag
Am Hofgarten 10
D-53113 BONN
Tel.: (49) 2 28 94 90 20
Fax: (49) 2 28 94 90 222
E-mail: bestellung@uno-verlag.de
http://www.uno-verlag.de

GREECE/GRÈCE
Librairie Kauffmann
28, rue Stadiou
GR-ATHINAI 10564
Tel.: (30) 1 32 22 160
Fax: (30) 1 32 30 320
E-mail: ord@otenet.gr

HUNGARY/HONGRIE
Euro Info Service
Hungexpo Europa Kozpont ter 1
H-1101 BUDAPEST
Tel.: (361) 264 8270
Fax: (361) 264 8271
E-mail: euroinfo@euroinfo.hu
http://www.euroinfo.hu

ITALY/ITALIE
Libreria Commissionaria Sansoni
Via Duca di Calabria 1/1, CP 552
I-50125 FIRENZE
Tel.: (39) 556 4831
Fax: (39) 556 41257
E-mail: licosa@licosa.com
http://www.licosa.com

NETHERLANDS/PAYS-BAS
De Lindeboom Internationale Publikaties
PO Box 202, MA de Ruyterstraat 20 A
NL-7480 AE HAAKSBERGEN
Tel.: (31) 53 574 0004
Fax: (31) 53 572 9296
E-mail: books@delindeboom.com
http://home-1-worldonline.nl/~lindeboo/

NORWAY/NORVÈGE
Akademika, A/S Universitetsbokhandel
PO Box 84, Blindern
N-0314 OSLO
Tel.: (47) 22 85 30 30
Fax: (47) 23 12 24 20

POLAND/POLOGNE
Głowna Ksiegarnia Naukowa
im. B. Prusa
Krakowskie Przedmiescie 7
PL-00-068 WARSZAWA
Tel.: (48) 29 22 66
Fax: (48) 22 26 64 49
E-mail: inter@internews.com.pl
http://www.internews.com.pl

PORTUGAL
Livraria Portugal
Rua do Carmo, 70
P-1200 LISBOA
Tel.: (351) 13 47 49 82
Fax: (351) 13 47 02 64
E-mail: liv.portugal@mail.telepac.pt

SPAIN/ESPAGNE
Mundi-Prensa Libros SA
Castelló 37
E-28001 MADRID
Tel.: (34) 914 36 37 00
Fax: (34) 915 75 39 98
E-mail: libreria@mundiprensa.es
http://www.mundiprensa.com

SWITZERLAND/SUISSE
BERSY
Route de Monteiller
CH-1965 SAVIESE
Tel.: (41) 27 395 53 33
Fax: (41) 27 395 53 34
E-mail: bersy@bluewin.ch

Adeco – Van Diermen
Chemin du Lacuez 41
CH-1807 BLONAY
Tel.: (41) 21 943 26 73
Fax: (41) 21 943 36 05
E-mail: info@adeco.org

UNITED KINGDOM/ROYAUME-UNI
TSO (formerly HMSO)
51 Nine Elms Lane
GB-LONDON SW8 5DR
Tel.: (44) 207 873 8372
Fax: (44) 207 873 8200
E-mail: customer.services@theso.co.uk
http://www.the-stationery-office.co.uk
http://www.itsofficial.net

UNITED STATES and CANADA/
ÉTATS-UNIS et CANADA
Manhattan Publishing Company
468 Albany Post Road, PO Box 850
CROTON-ON-HUDSON,
NY 10520, USA
Tel.: (1) 914 271 5194
Fax: (1) 914 271 5856
E-mail: Info@manhattanpublishing.com
http://www.manhattanpublishing.com

Council of Europe Publishing/Editions du Conseil de l'Europe
F-67075 Strasbourg Cedex
Tel.: (33) 03 88 41 25 81 – Fax: (33) 03 88 41 39 10 – E-mail: publishing@coe.int – Website: http://book.coe.int